As the ten houses in *Blueprint Affordable* strikingly demonstrate, budget-mindedness and beauty do not have to inhabit opposite sides of the architectural block. As unique as they are in their design, these houses all share one key attribute: From the very beginning, before their owners' dreams were transformed into exciting realities, everything from the floor plan to building materials and finishes was driven by limited financial resources.

Presented in a unique and friendly how-to format, *Blueprint Affordable* will leave you stunned to find that when frugality merges fearlessly with artistic freedom and creativity, the results can be dazzling.

Blueprint Affordable

Blueprint Affordable

How to Build a Beautiful House Without Breaking the Bank

Michelle Kodis

Gibbs Smith, Publisher
Salt Lake City

For Rich, once again—and always.

First Edition

08 07 06 05 04   5 4 3 2

Text © 2004 Michelle Kodis

Photograph copyrights as noted throughout

Published by

Gibbs Smith, Publisher

P.O. Box 667

Layton, Utah 84041

Orders: (1-800) 748-5439

www.gibbs-smith.com

Front and back cover photos: Jeffrey Jacobs, Architectural Photography, Inc.

Designed and produced by Kurt Wahlner

Printed and bound in China

Library of Congress Cataloging-in-Publication Data

Kodis, Michelle
   Blueprint affordable / Michelle Kodis.—1st ed.
     p. cm.
   ISBN 1-58685-307-4
   1. Architecture, Domestic—United States. 2. Architecture—United States—21st Century. 3. Building—Economic aspects. I. Title.
NA7208.2.K63 2004
728'.37'0973—dc22
                                   2003025036

Acknowledgments

My thanks and appreciation to

The architects, designers, builders, and homeowners who demonstrate through the examples in this book that they understand the power of a really great house.

The photographers whose images sing from these pages.

Gibbs Smith, a publisher on a mission for the printed word.

Suzanne Taylor, a dream of an editor.

Kurt Wahlner, for another beautiful book design.

Robert, Joan, and Steven Kodis, and the Cieciuch clan—my dear family.

My friends—Kendall Yaw Cieciuch, Marcia Cohen, Mary Duffy, Donna Fecteau, Ramona Gaylord, Susanna Hoffman, Jean Koch, Louise Redd, Susan Smilanic-Simpson, Susannah Smith, Rosemerry Wahtola Trommer, and Susan Viebrock.

Andrew and Brett Cieciuch—bright lights, excellent pals.

Violet and Roscoe, who take me on walks every day.

Contents

Introduction

Prospect, Colorado
Lawrence, Kansas
Chilmark, Massachusetts

Harbor Town, Tennessee

I F YOU DREAM of an architecturally distinctive house filled with graceful, beautiful materials, a space that has been customized to fit your lifestyle, but think you can't afford it—you have come to the right book.

My goal in the ten examples that follow is to help you discover the secrets of cost-conscious building and to show you, through descriptive stories accompanied by gorgeous color photographs, that cutting-edge residential design does not have to be prohibitively expensive. In fact, a thoughtful, well-crafted home that stands out like a rose in a field of daisies is not just for those with vast financial resources. What these architects and homeowners learned is that extraordinary but economical architecture was indeed within their reach, and by all accounts, they fully embraced these fresh and frugal approaches.

There are many ways to design and build on a budget; what follows are innovative and fun ideas that will save you money. The houses here represent a broad range of cost, style, and location, but they all share a common attribute: Before floor plans were finessed and materials selected, the undisputed star was the budget—and, most importantly,

9

the process of keeping it where it was supposed to be. To their immense credit, those who accepted the challenge found many clever ways to cut costs through resourcefulness, imagination, and even experimentation. The results, as you will see, are stunning, and the homes look as if they cost much more than they did.

Adhering to a strict budget is not always easy, though. In fact, it is a true labor of love and commitment. However, if you, your architect, and your contractor are willing to devote time to finding and putting into action the most cost-effective building methods and materials, your budget will survive—and you might even discover you have a bit of money left over for a splurge here and there. Whatever shape your dream takes and regardless of where you live, this book will guide you toward design and construction that places economic consideration on the same level of importance as aesthetics. I suggest you read the "Affordability Checklist" before you dive into the text, so you have a sense of the basic concepts.

The book's chapters are arranged in ascending order of cost per square foot. As you read, please remember this phrase: *relative affordability*. What this means is that on exclusive Martha's Vineyard, Massachusetts, a custom home built for $228 a square foot is a bargain, although in a locale with a comparatively lower cost of living, it might be viewed as expensive. Conversely, the $93-per-square-foot remodel of a Craftsman bungalow in Studio City, California, would be a great deal across a broad geographic spectrum. In some cases, the owners of the homes are themselves architects who drafted their designs and even acted as their own contractors. Despite these special circumstances, their limited budgets still relied on low-cost construction techniques and materials.

Also, for fair and accurate comparisons, the price listed at the beginning of each chapter refers to how much it cost to build or remodel the house on a per-square-foot basis. This figure does not include the purchase price of land or site work (excavation and landscaping) because such expenses can vary significantly by zip code, and the goal of this book is to demonstrate *what* you can build. The focus, then, is on the actual money-saving strategies: efficient floor plans, intelligent siting decisions, unconventional building systems, and budget-friendly materials and finishes.

My hope is that this book will stimulate your own inherent creativity and help you conceive a home that works on every level. I wish you adventure, enjoyment—and a healthy, happy bottom line!

MICHELLE KODIS

Affordability Checklist

Each of the ten chapters in this book delves into budget-conscious design and building techniques in detail, but here's a quick glimpse of the essential principles:

1. **Simple Floor Plan:** Keep your floor plan as modest as possible. An open "shell" plan, versus one with lots of rooms closed off with walls, is less expensive to build, and simple rectangles are always cheaper than curves or angles.

2. **Square Footage:** Watch your floor plan's footprint. Trimming square footage will also trim your budget.

3. **Simple Detailing:** Design your house to rely on straightforward elements versus those that are more complex and, thus, more expensive to build. To illustrate, square shed dormers are not as intricate as the gabled version—and both serve the same purpose. The words "simple detailing" should become part of your affordable-building vocabulary.

4. **Splurge Carefully:** Frugality is not about across-the-board sacrifice. You can splurge and still adhere to your budget, if you do so in a very limited application. If you love the look of expensive hardwood flooring but your budget won't permit a large quantity of it, use just a small patch of it in a special place.

5. **Materials:** Learn to appreciate the inherent elegance of basic, down-to-earth materials. Veneer plywood, concrete, drywall, steel, plastic laminate, and corrugated metal, to name just a few, are budget-friendly and, as the examples on these pages prove, anything but bland. And don't be afraid to use materials in unexpected—or unintended—ways.

6. **Recycle:** Incorporate recycled items into your cost-conscious dwelling—your budget will thank you, and you'll give new life to materials not quite ready to retire.

7. **Stock Sizes:** Opt for stock, off-the-shelf sizes, which cost less than their customized counterparts—and are just as functional and look just as good. Prefab materials and building systems (precast concrete foundations, cement board siding, prefab trusses) are also wise choices.

8. **Go Local:** Choosing locally available materials (such as woods) will lower shipping costs.

9. **Finishing:** If you can leave it exposed, do so. Expensive finish techniques can work against a budget, and in many cases, the beauty of structural materials can shine when they become an integral part of the palette. Rafters, joists, and trusses, for example, can be turned into prominent design elements at no extra cost.

10. **Climate:** Study your building site's climate and weather patterns, focusing on an architectural plan that shields the home from the elements. Doing so will add years to the life of your house and minimize maintenance and replacement costs.

11. **Basement:** If you can omit a basement, do so—you'll save thousands on excavation costs. If possible, build on a flat site, which will also decrease site preparation expenses.

12. **Long-term Planning:** Affordability should be approached both from the perspective of short-term and long-term benefits. Choosing materials for their durability, life span, and minimal maintenance requirements can sometimes cost more at the outset, but over time the savings will accrue.

13. **Utilities:** Pay attention to how utility costs will affect long-term affordability. Work with your architect to create a floor plan that encourages natural ventilation (to save on air conditioning) and that is economical to heat in the winter.

14. **Do it Yourself:** If you have the time, energy, and know-how, you can act as your own contractor and save significantly on labor costs. If you do hire a contractor, work closely with him on decisions about materials and finishes.

15. **Research:** Do your own research and purchase your own lighting fixtures, paint, carpet, and appliances instead of hiring an outside consultant to do so. If you're an experienced do-it-yourselfer, put your skills to use on the construction site—you'll save on labor and feel more connected to your new house.

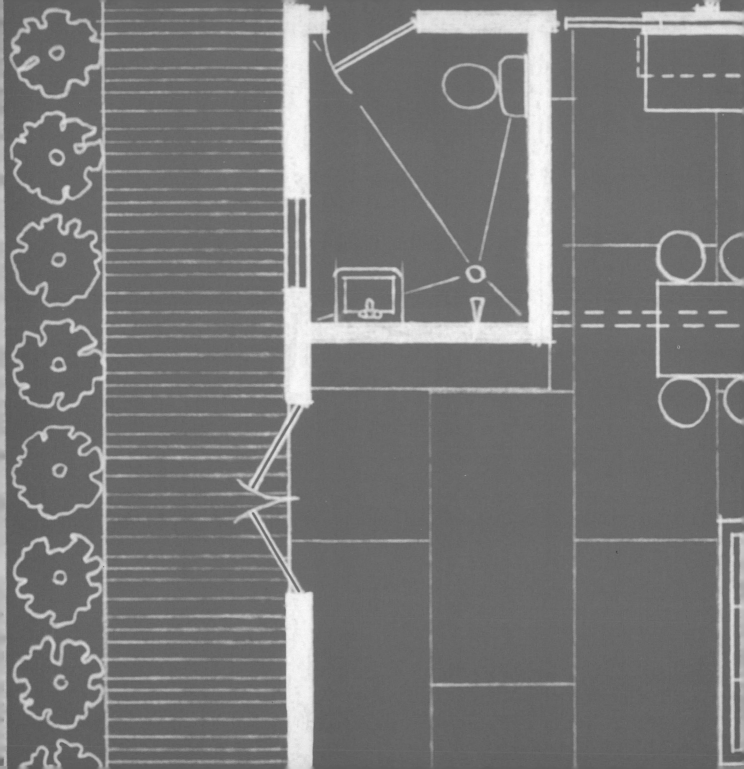

Blueprint # 1

*Affordable, off-the-shelf materials and a bit of
architectural experimentation reveal a winning
combination of charm and functionality.*

From Fish-and-Chips Stand
to Beachfront Home

Manhattan Beach, California

Cost per square foot: $55

Architects: José Abel Fontiveros and
Mariana Boctor, Sintesi Design Build

Photographs: Claudio Santini

Budget-Friendly Factors:

—careful consideration to issues of long-term maintenance and durability of materials

—off-the-shelf items and recycled hardware from
  restaurant supply stores

—birch plywood, concrete, structural steel, galvanized
  sheet metal, drywall, safety glass, combination of
  fixed and operable vinyl windows, sheet metal roof
  vent and cone

THIS MANHATTAN BEACH residence was suffer-
ing a steady decline and plagued by termites, wood
rot, and mold when José Fontiveros and Mariana
Boctor of the Santa Monica–based Sintesi Design
Build were invited to step in and work their
magic—as inexpensively as possible. Today the
home, lauded as a "box of art on the beach" by a
previous owner who spearheaded the initial reno-
vation, is a shining example of an economical
overhaul defined by a clean and casual style.

Fontiveros and Boctor had just received their
degrees from the UCLA Graduate School of
Architecture when they were handed the irre-
sistible opportunity of turning the building into a
comfortable but refined residence suited to beach
and family life. Ads placed at architecture schools

Steeply pitched gables inset with clapboard siding, stucco, a brick chimney, and bright
new double-paned vinyl windows combine to give the home its classic cottage façade.
The front windows are fixed instead of operable, a simple way to minimize costs.

had offered the home as a lab for "experimental design," and several interviews later, the owners found a match in Fontiveros and Boctor. Undaunted by the project's budgetary constraints, the pair welcomed the challenge, and their success is evident in how they combined materials from the lower end of the building spectrum in ways that look anything but cheap. According to Fontiveros, "The home was remodeled for the cost of what one prestigious architectural firm and contractor bid for the kitchen alone."

The first remodeling phase of the 965-square-foot, 1920s-era structure, originally built as a fish-and-chips stand and some years later converted into a summer getaway, focused on "ideas for fixing everything inexpensively," Fontiveros recalls. First, to

The home's exposed trusses and ceiling rafters were sandblasted for a textural effect, and 4 x 8 birch plywood panels, purchased for about $1,000 at a local Home Depot store, were installed as a subfloor that can be overlaid with another material. The materials palette unites plywood, metal, concrete, and glass, which are much less expensive than more traditional hardwood, marble, and stone. Exterior halogen flood lamp fixtures attached to the kitchen beam are an inexpensive lighting solution.

18

Beach Remodel

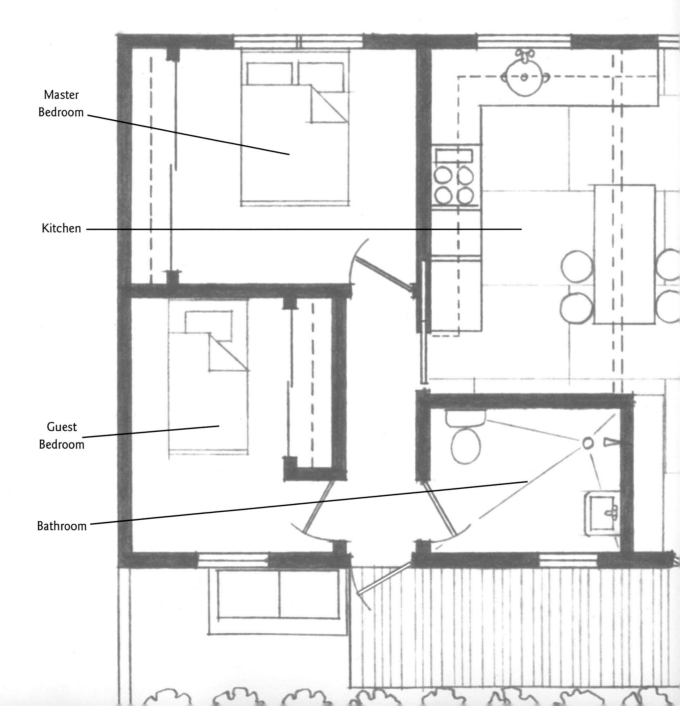

Master Bedroom

Kitchen

Guest Bedroom

Bathroom

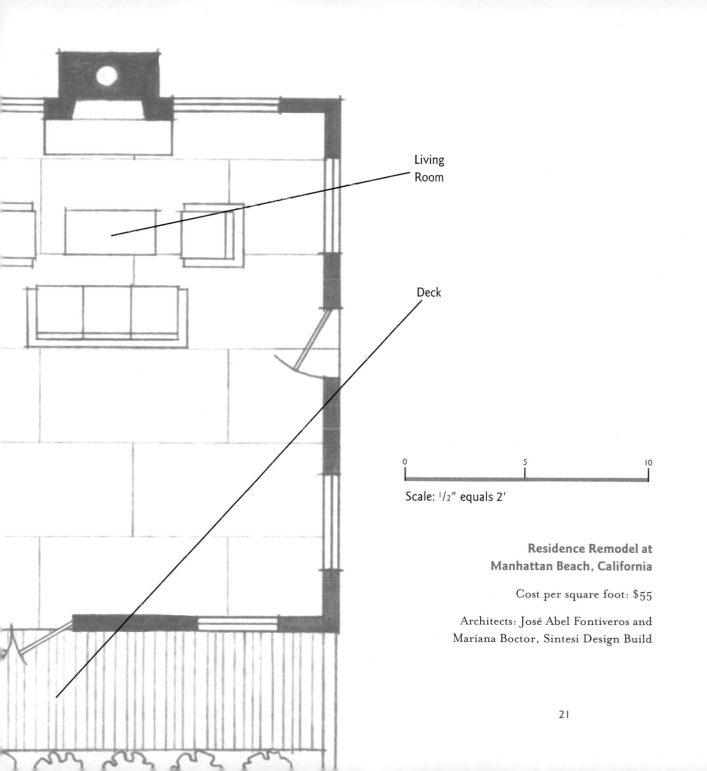

Living Room

Deck

0   5   10

Scale: $^1/_2$" equals 2'

**Residence Remodel at
Manhattan Beach, California**

Cost per square foot: $55

Architects: José Abel Fontiveros and
Mariana Boctor, Sintesi Design Build

21

reconfigure the tiny floor plan into a spacious combined kitchen/dining/living room, the architects suggested tearing down the decaying kitchen wall and shoring up the ceiling with a wood beam, left exposed for the dual purposes of saving money and introducing a rustic texture to balance the sleek industrial materials. Also on the agenda: adding windows and removing the rotting wormboard ceiling to reveal the handsome wood rafters, trusses, and steeply pitched gables.

Next, the duo embarked on an extensive bathroom makeover, cladding the walls and floor in durable lightweight concrete. From there, they updated the rest of the floors with birch plywood panels at a total cost of just $1,000, a thrifty alternative to

A Dutch front door brings light into the loft-like main living area, gutted to create a spacious combined living/dining room and kitchen. The removal of the kitchen wall allowed the small floor plan to breathe, and the beam installed to support the ceiling where the wall once stood adds architectural detail to the interior. The architects studied the concrete benches, drinking fountains and bathrooms and steel handrails of the "hardscape" along the nearby beach strand and connected the home to its environment using similar materials and designs.

Designed to harmonize with the kitchen, the concrete fireplace surround has a gas insert for economical heating, and the texture of the concrete contrasts nicely with the flat-finish walls and smooth plywood floors. The piece above the fireplace was made from steel I-beams and channels welded together and mounted to the wall to create a display of "built-in" art that can also serve as CD storage. A light behind the sanded Plexiglas piece adds depth to the unit.

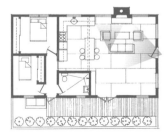

higher-end hardwoods. The plywood serves as a sub-floor that can, if desired, be covered with another material later. Confident they could revitalize the rest of the house with this proven combination of frugality and originality, the architects convinced the owner at the time to cancel her order for a new kitchen from a commercial supplier and instead go with their stream-lined and utilitarian concept, which features sealed concrete counters, a large antique copper pot embed-ded into the concrete and transformed into a sink complete with an industrial restaurant dishwashing-station faucet, and, instead of cabinets, an open shelv-ing system of plywood boards and green safety glass held together with metal rods and structural steel flat-bar "legs."

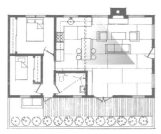

The kitchen is delineated both by the exposed beam and the island, which provides storage and seating and is equipped with electrical outlets. A perforated metal shelf, located beneath the counter, is a transi-tion between the kitchen and the fireplace. It is partially supported by Simpson hold-downs, which are normally used for wood framing, and the shelves are suspended from the cantilevered edge of the counter by thin steel rods. A custom hood was made using a prefabricated roof vent and sheet metal.

25

Items of Interest:

The Bombo barstools at the kitchen island, originally designed by Stefano Giovannoni and manufactured by Magis, are available at furniture stores and from online retailers of designer furniture.

The antique copper pot is from

Blackman Cruz
800 North La Cienega Boulevard
Los Angeles, CA 90069
(310) 657-9228

When present owner Paul Marchini bought the house in 2000, he had a clear goal. "My purpose was to take the house a step beyond what its previous owners had done," he says. "I wanted the feel of an easy beach house, one that needed little maintenance and wouldn't cost too much to fix up." He, too, called upon the talents of Fontiveros and Boctor with a request for a kitchen island that would provide storage, act as a dining table, and have the appearance of a piece of functional art. Crafted from metal, glass, concrete, and plywood, the island only *looks* expensive—a true testament to "what you can do affordably if you take the time to research the most inexpensive materials," Marchini points out.

Marchini kept his already lean budget on track by doing much of the additional work himself. He replaced the wood windows with a double-paned vinyl variety, a wise low-maintenance choice for the area's humid coastal climate. Realizing he didn't need to open every window in the house, he opted for fixed glass, versus the more expensive operable version, in the front windows, which trimmed his budget even farther. He also added a gas fireplace insert to the existing concrete surround.

Although today the house reflects the vision and effort of different owners, from the onset its makeover was directed by the same parameter: a strict budget. Thanks to plenty of creativity and a bit of architectural experimentation, the budget did not act as a hindrance, but rather resulted in a lively home that highlights the aesthetic qualities of simple but beautiful materials.

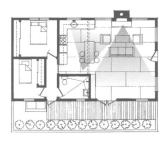

Overleaf:

The living room enjoys a strong connection to the outdoors thanks to paint-grade wood French doors in an affordable off-the-shelf 6-foot opening size; a custom door would have unnecessarily inflated the budget. Flat-finish drywall painted in a white high-gloss complements the darker tones of the wood.

The kitchen island showcases the sometimes-overlooked sophistication of the most basic of building materials: glass, metal, concrete, and plywood. The island's two lower cabinets are made of plywood and prefabricated metal grating, and feature recycled hardware from a restaurant supply store.

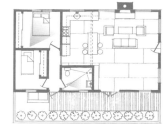

The current owner replaced a sliding window above the bed with a fixed piece of tinted glass that fosters privacy (important because another building sits close to the house) while allowing natural light into the room. Plywood floors and drywall are inexpensive but elegant.

The bathroom walls and floor were refinished in lightweight concrete. An old stainless steel, mirror-fronted medicine chest, found in a junkyard, stores personal items, while inexpensive, wall-mounted, galvanized sheet metal boxes keep towels and toiletries neatly stored. The porcelain sink is supported with brackets instead of a traditional pedestal to keep the unit off the floor for easier cleaning.

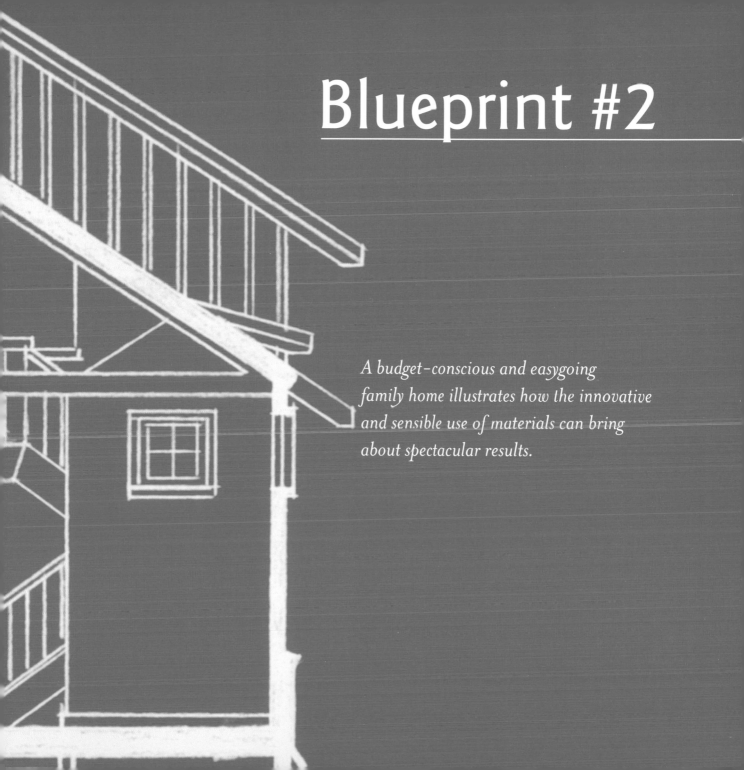

Blueprint #2

*A budget-conscious and easygoing
family home illustrates how the innovative
and sensible use of materials can bring
about spectacular results.*

Quaint
Ocean-View Cottage

Jamestown, Rhode Island

Cost per square foot: $80

Architect: Jim Estes, Estes/Twombly Architects

Photographs: Michael Mathers

Budget-Friendly Factors:

—simple, easy-to-build gable and shed forms designed to minimize labor costs and speed up construction schedule

—uncomplicated floor plan dominated by a basic rectangular main hall to eliminate the need for budget-inflating angles and walls

—rough-sawn T1-11 plywood siding, pine battens, eastern white pine clapboard siding, oak strip flooring, oak truss system, flat stock trim, painted steel, plaster-finish walls and ceilings, standard plumbing fixtures and window sizes

THE WELCOMING NATURE of this quaint and expressive Rhode Island home arises from its intimate size and spacious, well-lit interiors, while its budget-friendly nature reveals what can be accomplished with inexpensive off-the-shelf materials, straightforward forms, and special touches that, though easy on the bottom line, add up to a home with architectural flair.

The owners of the home knew what they wanted when they hired architect Jim Estes of Newport, Rhode Island–based Estes/Twombly Architects: a casual, free-flowing floor plan conducive to family life. To Estes, several challenges became apparent immediately: a narrow, sloping lot set back from the water, a marine climate—and a frugal budget. "The owners' expectations were not extravagant, and they were receptive to cost-saving ideas,"

Here, the interior "reading" of the home's two basic forms—the gable to the left and the dining room shed to the right—is evident. The home's many windows create a cheerful and inviting living space.

he says. "Those factors led the project from the very beginning."

Before he could embark on design, Estes first had to figure out how to position the home to secure the ocean views on a long-term basis and maximize the small building envelope. His solution was to orient the plan to diagonal views, avoiding a neighboring house and ensuring the views would not be compromised should that neighbor decide to build an addition to his house.

Estes' vision of the 2,200-square-foot house sprang from his knowledge that

The house is a basic gable form offset by varying shapes and materials that distinguish the lower and upper volumes. Using the sloping site to its best advantage, the architect seated the house on a plinth, which supports the deck and main living hall above and encompasses the basement below. Shed dormers, which are less expensive than more complex gable dormers, as well as a raised gable at one end of the house, unite familiar New England forms in a fresh and modern interpretation of the traditional cottage.

Jamestown Cottage

Lower Level

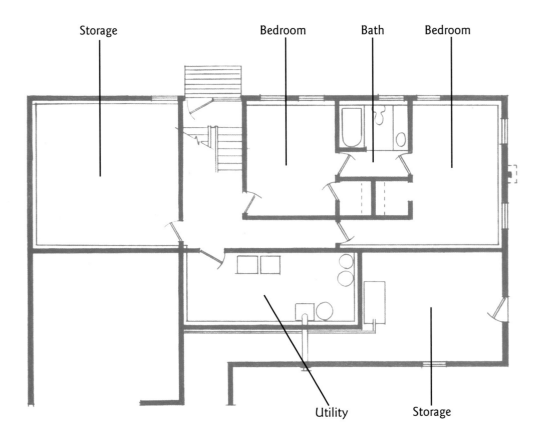

Storage

Bedroom

Bath

Bedroom

Utility

Storage

0 5 10 15 20

Scale: $^1/_2$" equals 6'

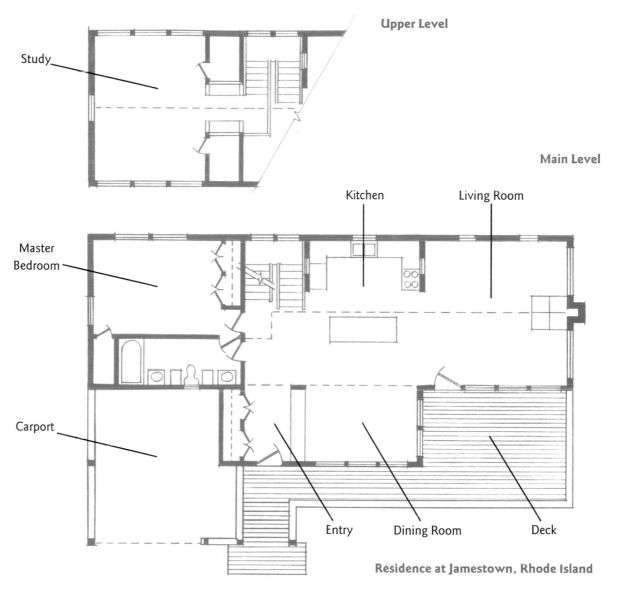

Upper Level

Study

Main Level

Kitchen

Living Room

Master
Bedroom

Carport

Entry

Dining Room

Deck

Residence at Jamestown, Rhode Island

Cost per square foot: $80

Architect: Jim Estes, Estes/Twombly Architects

simplicity in form and integral, versus applied, detailing both cuts costs and results in a home of distinction. To that end, he drew a basic rectangular main hall, or shell, topped it with a classic gable roof, and extended a shed roof from there to create the carport outside and provide a lower ceiling inside over the dining area. Three shed dormers pop out of the roof, bringing ambient light into the house and adding texture to the façade.

"There are no redundant spaces in this house," Estes explains. "It's all done in one big, open area, and that invariably saves money in any floor plan. Even in a place like this, which is pretty high-cost in terms of building, we were able to meet the budget by keeping the design of the house modest and relatively small."

In response to the sloped site and the clients' need for children's rooms, Estes seated the structure on a raised plinth, tucking the foundation into the slope and placing bedrooms at the lower open end and a storage and play area in the uphill section. In addition to providing extra square footage for rooms, the plinth lifts the primary living areas to take advantage of the setting. "As built, the house has better views than its waterfront neighbors because of the raised living hall," Estes says. "With right-of-way beach access, it is essentially a waterfront house at half the cost."

The next step was to find beautiful, affordable exterior materials that would stand up to the climate. For the plinth, Estes specified rusticated clapboard siding of locally milled, rough-cut 1 x 12 eastern white pine. Mitered corners on the plinth "make the high-relief clapboarding appear more solid and substantial, a proper base for the more detailed hall above," he points out. The exterior above the plinth is clad in rough-sawn T1-11 plywood siding, with rough-sawn pine battens placed twelve inches on center. Estes adds, "These are all Stick-style board-and-batten details common to other cottages in the neighborhood, but in combination with the clapboarded plinth, the hall tends to float above the base, especially at night."

The house is further defined by its generous window placement. Larger on the top part of the house, with divided lights in the upper portions, the windows open the home to the environment and, because they are off-the-shelf sizes, fit nicely into the budget. "Even with lower-cost houses, a relatively large part of the budget is often spent on glazing, especially on the south sides," Estes explains. "By doing this, you can extend the seasons, and by situating the deck correctly, as we have done here, the window and deck placement work together."

Inside, low-cost, long-lasting, eye-pleasing materials include plaster-finish walls and ceilings, flat-stock trim, standard oak strip flooring, an oak truss system, oak stairs, granite, painted steel, and standard plumbing fixtures. "This is one of the least expensive houses I've done," Estes says. "The key is to keep things simple and not get carried away with expensive details and finishes."

The straightforward shapes of the house are emphasized in this view: a gable with a shed extension that serves as a carport outside, forming the ceiling of the dining area inside. The windows in the house are either awning or double-hung instead of casements; the former are better in humid climates because they can be left open in light rains. Protective overhangs on the eaves are meant to extend the life of the siding and windows by reducing wear and tear from the elements.

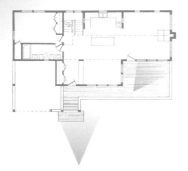

The carport, an economical alternative to an enclosed garage, transitions easily to the front door and deck. The brackets on the beam supporting the shed roof are both structural and decorative, and are continued as a design element in an eye-catching "frame" that announces the main entrance.

The north-facing side of the house has a simpler facade and less glass. The middle dormer, inset with an awning window, houses part of the staircase, and lower windows, kept free of mullions for a contrasting appearance, delineate the living areas of the basement. The plinth, sided in high-relief, eastern white pine clapboard accented with mitered joint corners, breaks up the mass of the building and stands out against the finer detailing of the upper portion, which is sided in rough-sawn plywood and pine battens.

The home's oversized double-hung windows stretched the limit of off-the-shelf dimensions and were a money-saving alternative to pricey custom sizes. The exposed structural rafters on the overhang add a level of richness to the exterior and, because they are integral to the structure, versus applied later, provide an economical way to impart architectural detail without inflating the budget. The deck flooring is affordable pressure-treated lumber. Inexpensive plastic Adirondack chairs complete the picture.

The chimney column, visible on the far green wall, runs along a notch cut into the wall.

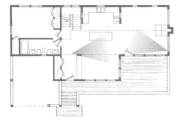

The main living areas of the house are contained in an open shell. The kitchen was placed within a simple plaster form to give it a subtle separation from the rest of the space instead of enclosing it entirely behind walls. The flooring is highly affordable oak strip, which is durable and brings color to the room, whose primary palette is the clean white of plaster-finish walls. The kitchen counter is granite, an elegant material that holds up to frequent use and adds nominal cost to a decorating budget.

A small loft at the top of the stairs serves as a continuation of the main hall and is a quiet place to relax.

The stair railing was budget-friendly thanks to low-cost painted steel, and economical to assemble because the pieces are separated at the corners and did not have to be precisely fitted.

47

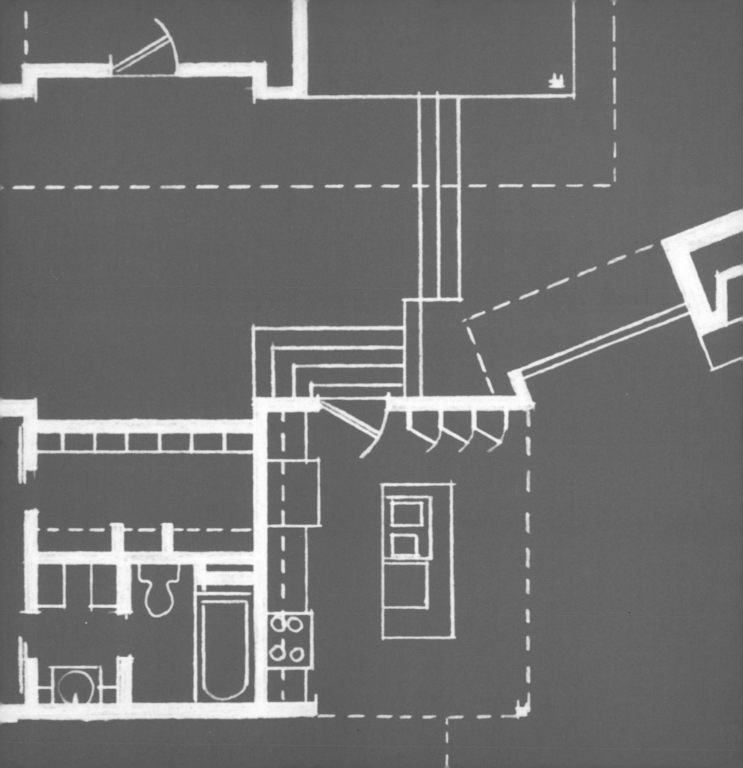

Blueprint #3

Contemporary and traditional forms meet in a home that is a showcase of inexpensive and beautiful materials.

A Contemporary Rendition
of a Traditional Design

Harbor Town, Tennessee

Cost per square foot: $88

Architect: Todd Walker, Archimania

Photographs: Jeffrey Jacobs, Architectural Photography, Inc.

At FIRST GLANCE, "Hannah's House," so named for the architect's young daughter, brings to mind the playfulness and carefree lightness of childhood. With its asymmetrical amplification of forms and blithe disposition, the house seems lifted from the pages of a storybook; indeed, this is where the do-gooders of the fairy-tale world might choose to live.

The house is in Harbor Town, a New Urbanist

Budget-Friendly Factors:

—owner served as general contractor and meticulously tracked expenses

higher-cost materials restricted to very limited applications and floor plan kept simple and open on first level

—glass block, Hardiplank, split-face concrete block, Sheetrock, plastic laminate, #2-grade maple flooring, birch plywood, cedar, western red cedar, mahogany, yellow pine, glulam, airplane cable, off-the-shelf fixtures, exposed structural forms

The living room's sloping wall is inset with operable windows of various sizes trimmed in inexpensive yellow pine. The television and fireplace unit is clad in birch plywood, and the concrete-block fireplace surround and the wall on the far right that holds up the truss both relate to the home's exterior walls. While the exterior masonry was left unfinished, inside it has been smoothed for a more refined look and to eliminate rough edges. Budget-conscious Sheetrock walls are found throughout the home.

community located on Mud Island on the Mississippi River near Memphis. Hannah's House, recognizable in its lines even as it announces a fresh perspective, gives a graceful nod to the more traditional tone of its neighborhood at the same time that it speaks to a present-day sensibility. "The house has a modern vernacular," explains owner and architect Todd Walker of the Memphis-based Archimania. "It offers a different twist on more familiar forms, and its overhangs, porches, and shapes represent what you might see, or have seen, elsewhere."

Budget firmly in hand, Walker and his wife, Patricia, knew what they wanted: a spacious custom home with generous outdoor living and play areas and pockets of privacy for retreat and work. Their wish list, stated clearly at the beginning of the process, was anything but extravagant: an open,

(continued on p. 62)

The width of the building site allowed for a clear delineation of the home's contrasting elements: a garage, fronted by a budget-friendly western red cedar door (stained to add contrast and color) and accented with a 6-foot overhang designed for sun protection; the house, with its unexpected lines, angled second-level wall, and simple, open porch; and a courtyard, which divides the two and serves as a play area and gathering place.

Memphis Rendition

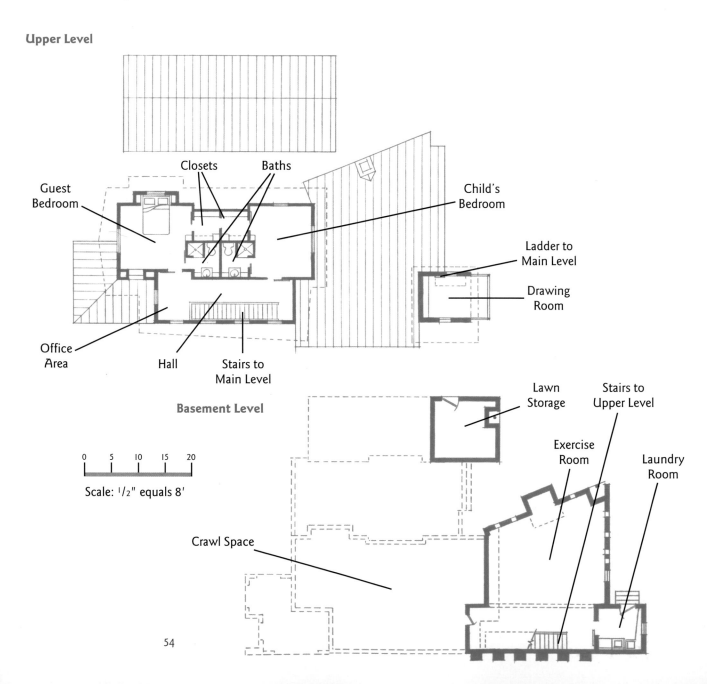

Upper Level

Closets

Baths

Guest
Bedroom

Child's
Bedroom

Ladder to
Main Level

Drawing
Room

Office
Area

Hall

Stairs to
Main Level

Basement Level

Lawn
Storage

Stairs to
Upper Level

Exercise
Room

Laundry
Room

0   5   10   15   20

Scale: $1/2$" equals 8'

Crawl Space

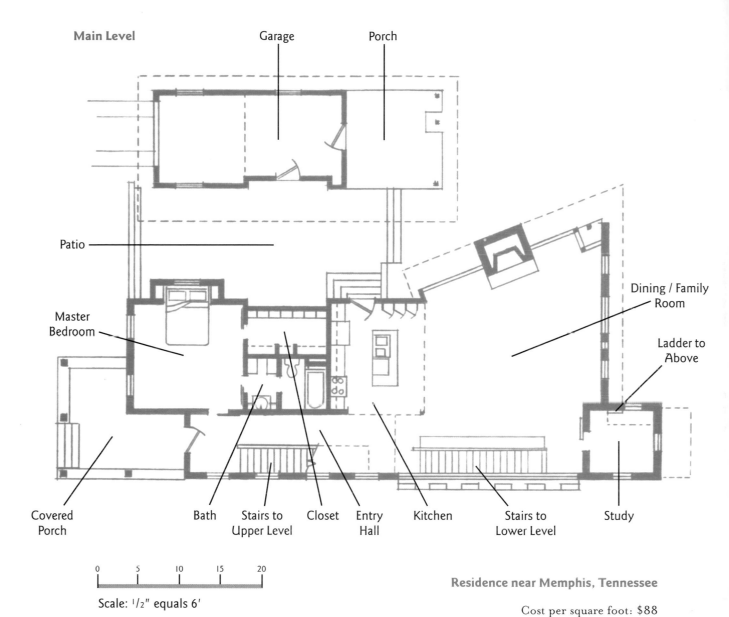

Main Level

Garage

Porch

Patio

Dining / Family Room

Master Bedroom

Ladder to Above

Covered Porch

Bath

Stairs to Upper Level

Closet

Entry Hall

Kitchen

Stairs to Lower Level

Study

0   5   10   15   20

Scale: ¹/₂″ equals 6′

Residence near Memphis, Tennessee

Cost per square foot: $88

Architect: Todd Walker, Archimania

The home's angled upper wall brings the facade up-to-date. Affordable exterior materials include tongue-and-groove shiplap cedar siding, painted white and applied in wider segments on the lower portion of the structure to create the perception of a strong base; Hardiplank siding; and glulam beams, left exposed beneath the overhangs to bring texture to the roof. Generous porch overhangs shade the house.

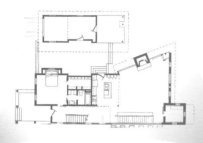

The architect recalled the historic lookout towers of the Mississippi River with this pop-out work studio. Here, the contrast between the front and back of the house is apparent, both from a design perspective and in materials that reflect a more industrial tone, namely split-face concrete block on the lower level wall and tower volume and commercial glass in the studio. Small windows allow light into the stairwell housed beneath the studio.

Having saved money elsewhere, the architect was able to buy expensive porch flooring. He chose Pau Lope, a Brazilian hardwood that is extremely durable and moisture-resistant, making it an intelligent option for a humid climate. The front door is made from affordable mahogany.

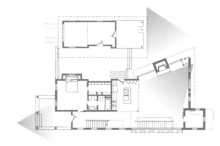

Overleaf:

A spectacular geometric window, supported by an aluminum frame painted red, is a piece of art built right into the house. Also visible is the home's pine truss beam, which bears on the steel beams that support the second floor. Left exposed to save money on concealing techniques, the truss is an affordable alternative to a concealed heavy steel beam, which costs more but performs the same job. The drawers below the red window are birch plywood.

This view from the porch highlights the transparency of the house, with the living room visible through large panes of commercial-grade glass. The space beneath the living room is an exercise room and playroom; inexpensive glass blocks "punched" into the concrete block bring ambient light into the room during the day and, when the room is lit at night, illuminate the yard. The chimney column is clad in split-face concrete block.

inviting family room that would combine living, dining, and kitchen areas; studio work spaces for both of them; an exercise and play room; plenty of deck and porch space; and a garage.

Beyond those essential components—and with the budget still driving their decisions—they began to envision the material features of the house that make it special and have since garnered it numerous honors and awards, including *Metropolitan Home* magazine's "Best New Home Design" in 2002, and several American Institute of Architects (AIA) citations for excellence. Those elements—a dramatic window trimmed in red, a tower section topped with a lookout, generous overhangs that provide sun protection and enhance the character of the facade, wood floors and doors, artful cabinetry, glass and cement block, and exposed structural forms—take the house into the realm of high design.

Walker was able to save on architectural costs because he designed the 3,040-square-foot, three-bedroom, two-bath house himself; additional expense was trimmed from the budget because he acted as his own general contractor. Working closely with subcontractors, he knew where every penny went. Had he not designed the home and been the contractor, he estimates the total cost would have been approximately 10 to 20 percent higher—still very affordable for the area.

The home's sloping site dictated its spatial dimensions. Walker discovered that the best use of the available building envelope was to separate the garage from the main house and extend the house back along the slope, which faces an industrial area across the river. Thanks to the width of the lot, Walker says, he was able to "carve out a space for a patio and play area, split the garage off, play down the scale of the house from the front, and allow breezes to flow through the property. It really worked well."

Birch plywood is prominent in the kitchen, and white plastic laminate, used for the island counter and several cupboard doors, adds visual variation at a nominal cost. The upper cabinet handles are asymmetrical cutouts instead of expensive hardware. The hardware on the lower cabinetry and pantry consists of stainless steel rods, which together cost just $150. The kitchen is delineated by a square of Brazilian cherry flooring, affordable because of its limited application. The maple dining table and chairs are from IKEA.

Walker had specific budget-conscious materials in mind when he designed the house, among them Hardiplank siding and board—an inexpensive, humidity-resistant material; split-face concrete block; birch plywood; cedar; mahogany; yellow pine; Sheetrock; glass block; plastic laminate; and #2-grade maple flooring. The home's floor plan, too, became an exercise in economy. For example, Walker placed the kitchen, dining area, and living room on the main floor in one open, wall-free space, a technique that saves construction dollars and has the added benefit of facilitating a connection, or "flow," as Walker puts it, between well-trafficked rooms of various functions. And, because budgets can easily inflate in the process of covering up the "insides" of a home, Walker chose to leave certain structural elements exposed, making them integral to the interior palette.

Because they were so frugal when selecting the majority of the home's materials, the Walkers were able to splurge occasionally without the risk of going over budget. Such splurges include the aforementioned red window in the living room, a square of Brazilian cherry flooring in the kitchen, and high-end—and extremely durable—Pau Lope wood for the front-porch flooring. "I was so tuned in to this budget that I knew the exact costs associated with the house from day one through to the finish," Walker says. "That also meant that I knew if I went below budget in one area, I could go over elsewhere and create places in the house for more expensive items. It's really about balance."

He concludes, "Often, the result of keeping to a tight budget ends up being more compelling because you have to consider creative ways to do things and put materials and design together in a way that isn't typical."

The home's flooring is a combination of #1- and #2-grade maple, the latter of which is less expensive and also darker and less regular in grain, which in turn imparts a greater degree of color variation, character, and warmth to the space. The painted steel stairway has solid maple treads and low-cost quarter-inch airplane cable for rails; the cable can be purchased at home supply stores.

The headboard in the bedroom fits neatly into an alcove and is flanked by built-in birch plywood storage cubbies. The alcove was an inexpensive way to extend the dimensions of the room.

The birch plywood cubby system is repeated in the bathroom, with small drawers and vented hampers beneath the drawers. The counter is crafted of white plastic laminate. Standard off-the-shelf fixtures and a basin by Kohler complete the look.

Blueprint #4

A 1920s-era house gets new life with a nature-inspired selection of cost-effective and recycled materials and a "tree house" master bedroom.

An Innovatively Remodeled California Bungalow

Studio City, California

Cost per square foot: $93

Architect: John Sofio, Built, Inc.

Photographs: Courtesy of Built, Inc.

I**N A COMPELLING EXAMPLE** of "blurring the lines between the indoors and the outdoors," as architect John Sofio explains it, this exquisitely remodeled and expanded Craftsman bungalow near Hollywood embraces its setting and boasts a new second-story master bedroom reminiscent of a tree house.

Budget-Friendly Factors:

—structural elements left exposed, versus covered, for financial savings and to add "free" design features to the exterior and interior

—focus on how climate and weather patterns would affect the home's longevity and utility costs, and on creating a design that would provide efficient natural ventilation, thus lowering air-conditioning expenses

—spruce siding, T1-11 plywood siding, stucco, asphalt roofing (good long-term investment), salvaged Douglas fir, glulam, red oak floors, old stone paving pieces used for fireplace, drywall, walnut veneer, steel cable

Spruce siding, Douglas fir windows, a glulam beam, T1-11 plywood siding on the exterior of the sliding doors, and a brick chimney merge in a celebration of the colors and textures of nature—all at the lowest possible cost. When opened, the window of each sliding door frames a square of the yellow stucco in a pop art fashion. Left uncovered to mirror the rich wood of the upper-level windows, the glulam beam was cut at the same angle as the exposed rafter tails for architectural consistency. The decking is Douglas fir, salvaged from the original structure and finished with a heavy-body stain.

When Derrick Drymon and Nancy Moscatiello hired Los Angeles–based Sofio to reconfigure the 700-square-foot bungalow to accommodate their growing family, they presented him with creative freedom—and a slim budget. Sofio, however, was undeterred by the financial limitations; experience told him he could transform the house at a reasonable cost and still express a sense of architectural and aesthetic discovery.

Originally built in the 1920s as part of an artists' colony, the home sits at the bottom of a glen, under a rich canopy of foliage. Allured by the thought of being up in the

Stucco, here in a custom yellow pigment, is durable and easy to install and maintain, and a steel-trowel finish gives it a smooth appearance. A Dutch front door made from Douglas fir aerates the interiors and doubles as a window. The Douglas fir deck railing is strung with low-cost steel cable, and the chimney, made from salvaged bricks, stabilizes the house during earthquakes.

Studio City Bungalow

Main Level

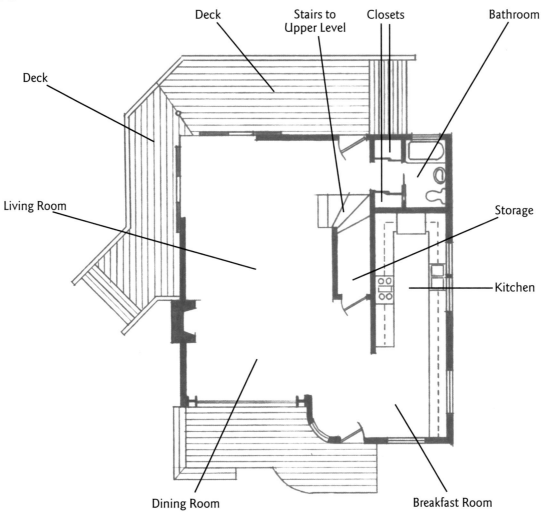

Deck

Stairs to
Upper Level

Closets

Bathroom

Deck

Living Room

Storage

Kitchen

Dining Room

Breakfast Room

Upper Level

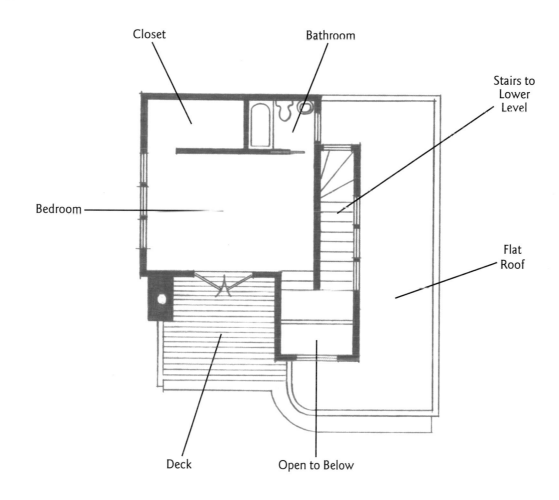

Closet

Bathroom

Stairs to
Lower
Level

Bedroom

Flat
Roof

Deck

Open to Below

0   5   10   15   20

Scale: $^1/_2$" equals 5'

Residence Remodel at Studio City, California

Cost per square foot: $93

Architect: John Sofio, Built, Inc.

trees, the owners requested that the master bedroom look and feel like a refined tree house. And, they wanted a main living space that didn't feel cramped and had a strong connection to the environment. After analyzing the budget requirements and spending hours perched on the roof scrutinizing everything from the site's wind patterns to the arc of the sun, Sofio conceived a graceful, site-sensitive, 650-square-foot expansion characterized by vivid colors borrowed from nature, simple and affordable materials, and a clear link between interior and exterior spaces.

The home's revamped floor plan features a spacious main living area, the result of knocking down walls to combine the existing living room with a first-floor bedroom. Still cozy, the room's personality can be quickly altered, thanks to a cantilevered door that swings up effortlessly like a garage door and, on the opposite side of the room, two doors set on tracks that open a back corner of the house, obliterating physical boundaries and wisely taking advantage of California's abundant sunshine and reliably good weather. The master bedroom, with its 30-inch roof overhangs, appears to hover delicately over the lower level.

Although the red cantilevered door weighs nearly 1,600 pounds, its streamlined design makes it easy to open and close and, thanks to on-site assembly, it was a bargain at $1,000—thousands less than an off-site assembly. Mixing operable and fixed windows also brought savings. The curved fixed-glass corner window was made on-site from separate pieces of glass butted together; it was just $200, whereas a custom single-piece window would have cost significantly more.

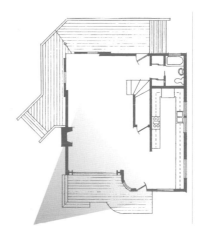

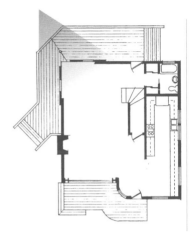

The living room easily transforms into a see-through indoor/outdoor space with the simple action of sliding the track doors open and lifting the large door at the front of the house. The sliding doors extend the boundaries of the lower level and, as a bonus, were kind to the budget. Supported by a structural steel pipe column, the glulam beam soars out of the room, integrating the interior and exterior.

With each project, Sofio looks for ways, some of them subtle, to achieve low-cost—or even no-cost—architectural distinction. "It's important to think about what you can do without doing more," he says. "If you can expose the structure of the house, you can reduce its maintenance and, therefore, expense, and give it a palette of color and texture. Leaving key features exposed costs nothing but can have a beautiful effect. I call it instant architecture!"

This concept is revealed throughout the building, from its visible rafter tails and framing to a bare structural pipe column and the cantilevered door's structural steel moment frame (a special frame to resist horizontal forces), all of which set the stage for the home's vernacular, which Sofio describes as "organic industrial." Design doesn't get in the way of function in this house, however. To illustrate, the moment frame contributes to the style of the facade, but more importantly it can withstand earthquake tremors. Similarly, the chimney's verticality is an integral piece of the overall composition—and

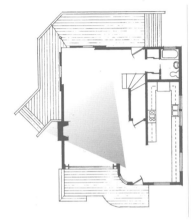

The yellow walls of the sunny and spacious living room mimic the exterior stucco, and stained red oak floors are as beautiful as white oak but less expensive. The variety of materials in the home speaks to its "organic industrial" vernacular: in this room alone, the architect specified everything from natural wood to a steel pipe column.

its sheer-resisting properties prevent the house from shaking during a quake.

One of Sofio's primary methods for keeping this budget as low as possible was to find fresh uses for old materials—namely Douglas fir boards and stone paving pieces—salvaged during construction. Surprisingly, perhaps, the original house was built with recycled Douglas fir to begin with, so "the current version of this house features twice-recycled materials," Sofio points out, adding, "we wanted to preserve and continue that legacy." The ceilings of the master bedroom showcase the home's original studs, which Sofio and his crew milled into appropriately sized planks. Recycled Douglas fir also graces the deck, the eaves, and the stairway to the second floor. The architect discovered yet another advantage to this application: The wood's natural aging process made it stronger than new material, eliminating the need for finish—which in turn saved money. Patio bricks were used for the two-story chimney, and the fireplace is comprised of stone also from the property.

Other budget-friendly materials include spruce siding (the least expensive you can buy without going to a man-made product); stained red oak floors (less expensive than white oak), T1-11 plywood siding, walnut veneer, asphalt roofing (with its life span, it is cheaper in the long run), stucco, and steel cable. Furthermore, Sofio took other factors into consideration to

The fireplace provided a way to reuse the brick paving stones salvaged from the original house during construction. Meant to resemble a mineshaft opening, it also features a recycled Douglas fir mantel and sides, an inexpensive stone manteltree, and metal straps. Attached at a crisp 90-degree angle, the fireplace appears to "slice" into the wall.

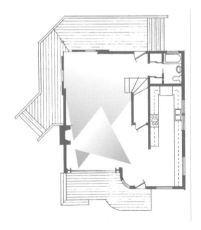

A glulam beam with a clear finish and exposed original framing instill architectural detail at nominal expense. The square fixed window in the sliding door brings light into the room and was less expensive than an operable version. The inside of the door is clad in thin strips of walnut veneer, another cost-conscious option.

minimize costs, such as carefully weather-proofing the house and positioning it so that its windows and door openings are protected from the elements, reducing wear and tear and, thus, upkeep. He also ensured the presence of natural ventilation to help lower air-conditioning bills.

Overall, Sofio's methods prove that a home built on a budget can have everything its more expensive peer might have—the only difference being that its inhabitants have money left over for other uses.

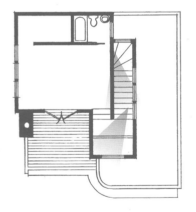

The first few stairs leading to the master bedroom are wood, while the rest are covered in inexpensive carpet, a simple technique that saved money because carpet tends to be cheaper than wood. The 14-foot handrail was crafted from an old beam left over after construction.

The stairway incorporates the home's original Douglas fir, shown here in the newel post, railings, and ceiling planks. Inexpensive steel cabling complements the natural hues and texture of the wood.

The master bedroom "tree house" is cozy and inviting. Due to the beautifying effects of the natural aging process, the Douglas fir ceiling planks needed no finish. The low ceiling is constructed like a marriage canopy, and the doors open to a small deck.

Redwood shingles lend a natural contrast to the man-made elements of the house. Because its series of hip roofs is visible from the street, the architect mixed black and charcoal asphalt shingles, which together are livelier and lighter than a single color. Although initially more costly than some other roofing materials, asphalt has an impressively long life span and requires minimal upkeep, making it less expensive over time.

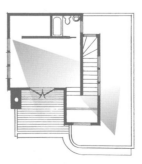

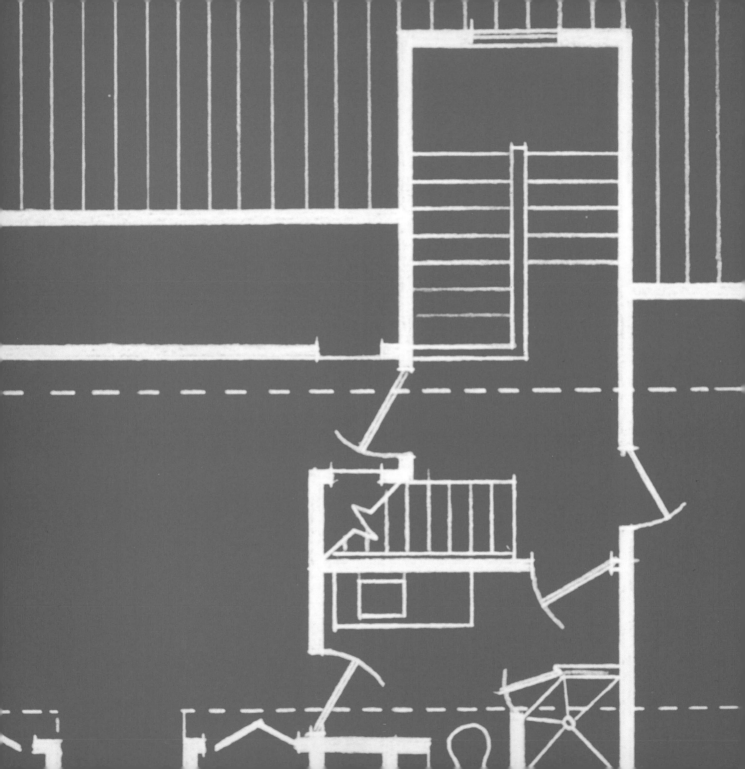

Blueprint #5

A cozy cabin in the country incorporates affordable and attractive materials within a casual, low-maintenance floor plan.

Rustic Elegance Beside the River

Bath Springs, Tennessee

Cost per square foot: $100

Architect: Carson Looney, FAIA, Looney Ricks Kiss Architects

Photographs: Terry Sweeney

THE WEEKEND CABIN designed and owned by architect Carson Looney is a graceful combination of old and new, natural and man-made, rustic and modern—all in just 1,500 square feet and with a budget of $100 per square foot.

Located on the picturesque banks of the Tennessee River, the cabin, with its inviting, well-scaled interiors and spacious wraparound porch, speaks to lazy summer days and energetic family gatherings.

Budget-Friendly Factors:

—rectangular floor plan that allows the use of stock versus custom materials, thus reducing the duration and cost of labor

—focus on a comfortable, family-oriented house with minimal maintenance requirements, which brings long-term savings

—standard-size treated pine support timbers, PVC shutters, concrete-filled support tubes, Hardiplank siding, plastic laminate, commercial-grade carpet, fixed-glass windows, gypsum board ceilings, tongue-and-groove pine walls, galvanized metal, aluminum-clad windows, low-E glass, exposed fireplace flue, pine stair treads, prefabricated fireplace

Impervious to freeze/thaw cycles, cost-conscious Hardiplank siding is low-maintenance, whereas more expensive wood demands regular upkeep. The galvanized metal fireplace flue was left exposed to save money and add another element to the home's exterior palette, and the shutters were made to look like traditional wood shutters but are inexpensive and moisture-resistant PVC.

Best of all, the house is as low-maintenance as they come, easy upkeep being one of Looney's primary goals. "In our family home, which was built by my great-great-grandfather, something always needs to be repaired," he says. "I wanted this house to impose no burden and be hassle-free for everyone who spends time in it."

Looney's other goal was spending money wisely, and he tailored his budget around modest architecture and affordable, long-lasting materials. He conceived the house as a rectangle—more cost-effective than an L-shape or other more complex configuration and equally livable—and capped it with an appropriately pitched galvanized-metal roof accentuated with three shed dormers and a viewing tower. The ample roof overhangs form the

The home reveals the appeal of clean lines and the unexpected juxtaposition of materials. A galvanized-metal roof spans the rectangular form—raised aboveground as a precaution against potential flooding—and is punctuated by shed dormers that "cut" into the roof, bringing drama to the facade and pulling the dormer windows farther into the rooms. The porch is two feet lower than the raised main level to give it more depth and a sense of separation, and a raised viewing tower caps the structure and enhances the home's verticality. Plenty of aluminum-clad windows connect the interiors to the surroundings.

Tennessee Weekender

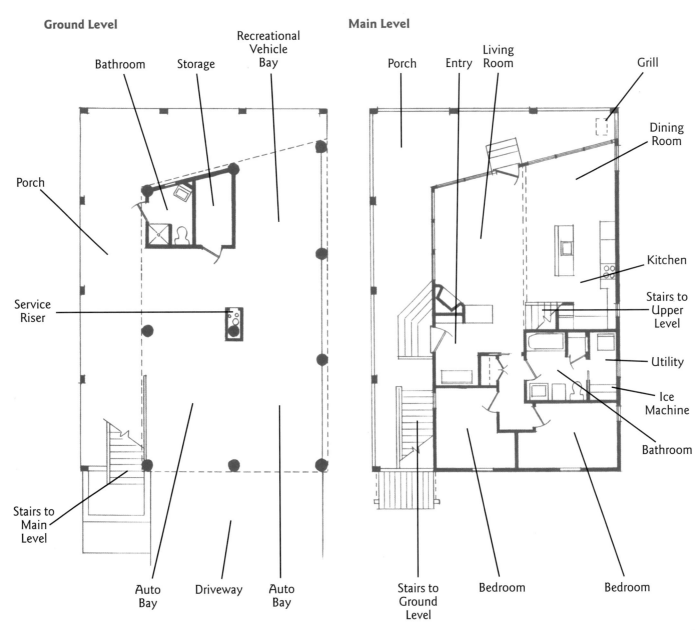

Ground Level

Bathroom

Storage

Recreational Vehicle Bay

Porch

Service Riser

Stairs to Main Level

Auto Bay

Driveway

Auto Bay

Main Level

Porch

Entry

Living Room

Grill

Dining Room

Kitchen

Stairs to Upper Level

Utility

Ice Machine

Bathroom

Stairs to Ground Level

Bedroom

Bedroom

Upper Level

Master Bedroom

Window Seat

Storage

Stairs to Main Level

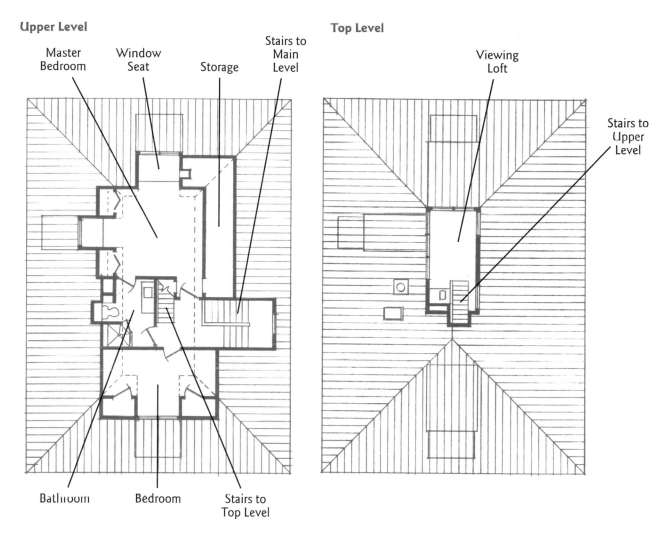

Bathroom

Bedroom

Stairs to Top Level

Top Level

Viewing Loft

Stairs to Upper Level

0 5 10 15 20

Scale: ¹/₂″ equals 7′

Residence at Bath Springs, Tennessee

Cost per square foot: $100

Architect: Carson Looney, FAIA, Looney Ricks Kiss Architects

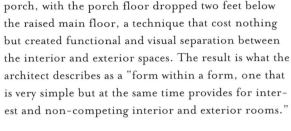

porch, with the porch floor dropped two feet below the raised main floor, a technique that cost nothing but created functional and visual separation between the interior and exterior spaces. The result is what the architect describes as a "form within a form, one that is very simple but at the same time provides for interest and non-competing interior and exterior rooms."

The home's floor plan accommodates standard-size lumber, including 12-foot floor joists. "With any home, I think about economy and how that relates to materials," Looney explains. "I designed this house around as much standard-length lumber as possible. When you don't have to cut lumber to fit the floor plan because you've thought ahead and designed the floor plan to fit the lumber, you save money on labor and reduce material waste."

Concrete-filled Sonotubes support the home's platform and provide textural variety. Stairs crafted from standard 2 x 12 pine boards lead to the porch and are protected by an overhang of treated pine covered with galvanized roofing and suspended with one-inch steel rods. Exposing the rafters at the cornice edges saved money on materials and labor and added another subtle detail. To provide contrast to the man-made materials, the architect used inexpensive 8 x 12 treated pine support timbers. The locally fabricated porch railing is durable painted steel.

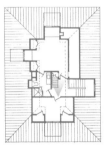

The pine treads on the stairs leading to the viewing loft were purchased for a significant discount because they had been cut as extras for other construction projects and were sold as leftovers. The walls are clad in #1 tongue-and-groove pine, one of the least expensive woods on the market. An elegant iron railing complements the pine walls and antique heart pine flooring.

Wood walls give the cabin a rural elegance and balance the contemporary materials and lines of the kitchen. Paring down the kitchen imagery allowed it to coexist in the main living area without overpowering it. Inexpensive gypsum board ceilings offset the cost of the slightly more expensive wood walls.

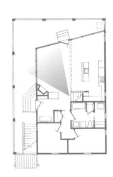

Antique heart pine built-ins house the television and fireplace, which occupy a corner of the living room and block the view to the foyer, located beyond the wall and visible through the niche above the television. The prefabricated fireplace features cast-iron panels designed to look like real brick. Because the raised house couldn't support a masonry fireplace, this prefab model was a safe and attractive alternative.

Affordable fixed glass attached directly to the window frames to maximize the surface area of the glazing opens the living area to views of the river, and double-hung windows and a patio door provide ventilation. Combining fixed and operable glass saved money while serving two key purposes: views and air circulation. The flooring is 18 x 18 porcelain tile, a hardy material in a color meant to camouflage the inevitable effects of people and pet traffic.

Due to the potential for flooding, the house sits above ground and is supported by substantial 18-inch reinforced concrete-filled tubes called Sonotubes. Inexpensive and strong, the columns, which were fabricated on-site, have an industrial appearance that appealed to Looney, who wanted a compositional variety of texture on the home's exterior. Hardiplank siding was used in lieu of the more maintenance-intensive cypress or cedar. Painted to look like wood, the Hardiplank brought the general desired character and was a better long-term choice. Other low-maintenance, budget-friendly, and eye-catching exterior elements include 8 x 12 treated pine timbers installed to support the main floor and porch roof; aluminum-clad windows instead of wood, which needs regular care, and PVC fashioned into shutters and painted to resemble wood.

Inside, the architect's budget-savvy choices include an instant gas hot-water heater, which helps keep utility bills to a minimum, low-E glass, and plenty of fixed glass. "It's rare that you would open all the windows in a room," he explains, "so fixed glass is a solution that maximizes the views and reduces costs." The orientation of the windows and porch minimizes heat gain during the summer, reducing cooling costs. Plastic laminate kitchen cabinets with granite tops, tongue-and-groove pine walls, gypsum board ceilings, porcelain tile, commercial-grade carpet, and white shower tiles combine to impart a relaxed look without "making this one of those cabins that overwhelms you with its overdone 'cabin' features," Looney says.

His suggestions for not breaking the bank illustrate the virtues of practicality and restraint. "First, throw away the blinders and think about how you are really going to live in the house, and not about what you think you'd like—this kind of balance is key," he says. "Also, don't let your basic design eat up all the budget; instead, build a structure and layer on finishes as your budget allows. It's important to focus on things people utilize, experience, and touch, so if you save money elsewhere, such as with simple, uncomplicated architecture, you can do this and have a home of true beauty."

A kitchen island made of painted pine and topped with granite features a storage niche beneath the upper shelf to hide clutter. A single sink, versus a double, saved money and maximized the usable counter space. Commercial-grade plastic laminate cupboards, drawers, and refrigerator cabinet, all equipped with stainless steel handles, are affordable and beautiful options—and are easy to clean. The small niche under the stair houses a pantry, microwave, and storage area.

A restored dry sink, made of pine stained a deep black and inset with a modern Kohler bowl, serves as a vanity. The architect saved enough money with budget-friendly 6 x 6 white bathroom tiles that he was able to purchase a higher-end shower door. The pine door was designed and built by the architect and his contractor.

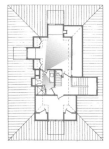

Painted tongue-and-groove pine walls give the master bedroom a rustic warmth, and commercial-grade carpet will hold up to the rigors of country living. The draperies can be pulled across the dormer bay to form an extra sleeping area, and built-in shelves are a tidy way to store books.

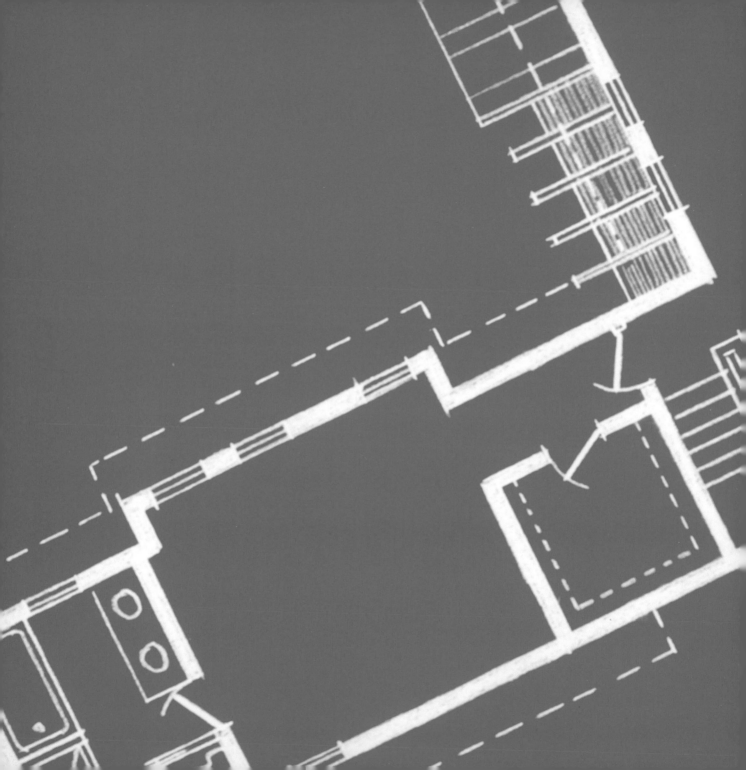

Blueprint #6

A New Urbanist community embraces fresh design and reveals the possibilities to be discovered even with a limited budget.

A Casual House in a New Kind of Neighborhood

Prospect, Colorado

Cost per square foot: $115

House Design: Mark Sofield, Prospect Town Designer

Photographs: Ron Pollard

THIS CONTEMPORARY HOME on Colorado's Front Range was selected for this book as much for its location as for its sensible, cost-effective design. The house is part of the New Urbanist community of Prospect, one of several across the country that offer attractive alternatives to the conventional American suburb, whose defining attributes are often oversized yards, prominently displayed garage doors, and wide streets that separate neighbors.

Budget-Friendly Factors:

—spare applications of materials to keep expenses to a minimum and create a house with an elegantly minimalist charm

—selected exterior and interior structural elements left exposed to reduce materials and labor costs

—tempered hardboard siding, metal barn roofing, basic framing lumber, poured-concrete patio and porch floors, welded-steel porch railings, Baltic birch plywood flooring and trim, Sheetrock, slate tile, off-the-shelf lighting fixtures, concrete counters

The home's street-side facade evokes the historic mining structures found throughout Colorado. Affordable and long-lasting materials include tempered hardboard siding, here painted green; poured-concrete porch support columns; welded-steel porch railings inset with industrial steel-mesh panels; painted wood windows; and a sturdy metal roof.

Prospect's blocks are connected by narrow tree-lined avenues that link detached homes, townhouses, courtyard houses, apartments, and live/work lofts—all in a broad range of architectural expression, from traditional to modern—to shops, offices, parks, and other public amenities. People live and work in Prospect, where the daily commute is headache-free and the lifestyle is decidedly nonconformist; certainly, those who live here are well aware they're going against the grain of the mainstream, and that pleases them immensely. Prospect has won numerous awards, including the state's coveted Governor's Smart Growth Award in 1996, a testament to the innovation of developer Kiki Wallace, who took the eighty acres owned by his family—land that previously served as a tree farm—and built a neighborhood that actually feels like a neighborhood.

Mark Sofield, Prospect's supervising designer and a resident of the community, created this house in a style dubbed "mineshaft modern" by local residents for its reflection of

The garage, with its flat tempered hardboard door and poured-in-place concrete walls, faces the alley and is the base for a rental apartment. The stairway is made from painted framing lumber, a low-cost alternative to a more expensive material, and the structural steel pipe column at the top of the stair was left unadorned for a minimalist appearance and to prevent it from intruding into the small landing. To protect the owners' privacy, the apartment windows are focused away from the courtyard.

Prospect Casual

Main Level

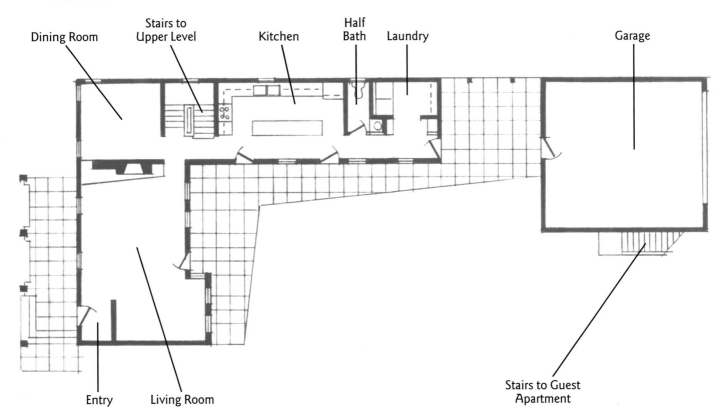

Dining Room

Stairs to
Upper Level

Kitchen

Half
Bath

Laundry

Garage

Entry

Living Room

Stairs to Guest
Apartment

Scale: $^1/_2$" equals 7'

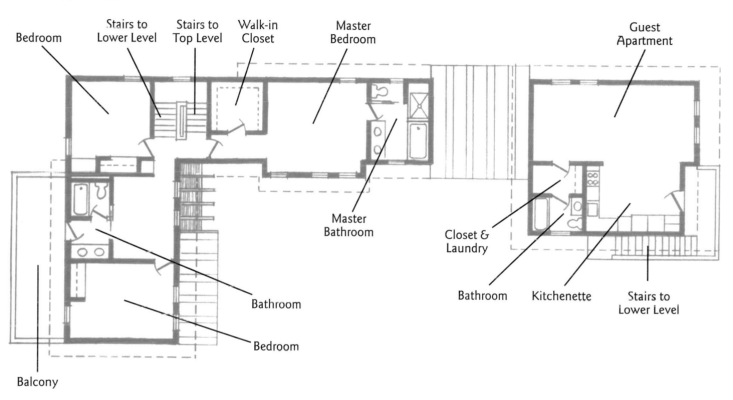

Upper Level

Bedroom

Stairs to Lower Level

Stairs to Top Level

Walk-in Closet

Master Bedroom

Guest Apartment

Master Bathroom

Balcony

Bathroom

Bedroom

Closet & Laundry

Bathroom

Kitchenette

Stairs to Lower Level

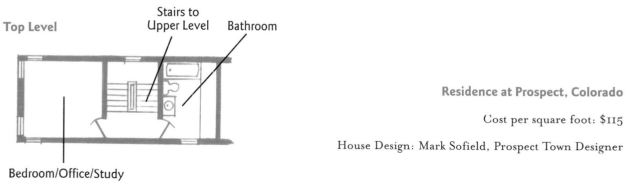

Top Level

Stairs to Upper Level

Bathroom

Bedroom/Office/Study

Residence at Prospect, Colorado

Cost per square foot: $115

House Design: Mark Sofield, Prospect Town Designer

The entry, with its light-filtering transom window, is inviting in nature and intimate in scale. An economical Baltic birch plywood shelf, which forms part of a partition wall meant to block views into the interior living spaces, was crafted from leftover scraps trimmed from flooring squares; recycling the excess material saved money and minimized waste.

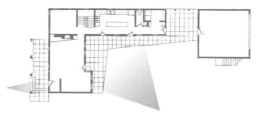

The back of the L-shaped house forms a private courtyard. Here, an ample window placement takes advantage of the area's abundant sunshine, while wood trellises shade the interiors from the intense summer sun. The second-level bay to the right houses the master bedroom; this pop-out was an inexpensive way to increase the size of the room. Leaving the rafters exposed eliminated finishing costs and brought visual variation to the roof, and the generous width of the lap siding helped to balance the building's proportions.

iconic Colorado forms, namely agriculture and mining structures. Built for $115 per square foot, this unique 2,477-square-foot home rivals many standard-production houses in the area, which can start at $125 per square foot and go up from there. Although not all of Prospect's homes fall into this range, this house was conceived specifically around the concept that budget-conscious architecture can be beautiful and comfortable.

Sofield began with the site: 48 feet wide by 100 feet deep, with its long axis oriented north and south. The front of the house faces north, while the back, with its southern exposure, gets plenty of sun, making it a natural location for ample window placement that doesn't compromise privacy. The L-shaped building wraps around the north and east sides of the lot to form a courtyard tucked behind the house; the back windows look out onto this yard. "Privacy is a big deal in Prospect," Sofield points out. "The houses are close together and near the street, so giving this home zones of privacy was a key consideration. The courtyard helps achieve that."

Built on three levels to allow the top floor to capture views of the nearby Rocky Mountains, the house has a spaciousness that belies its tight footprint. Sofield envisioned a family home whose "activity zones

(continued on p. 121)

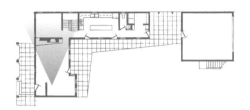

An inexpensive Sheetrock wall houses a gas fireplace insert and separates the living room from the dining room without blocking them off completely from each other. The plate steel mantel wraps around the top and sides of the fireplace insert, and a slate tile hearth edged with raw steel strapping is wide enough for sitting or for displaying objects.

A built-in shelf made from excess flooring material is a tidy way to display belongings and hold a reading lamp. Sheetrock walls and low-cost plywood baseboard trim (to match the flooring) kept costs on track, and exposed framing brought texture to the rooms without inflating the budget.

A fourth bedroom in the home was converted into an office/study. Located on the third floor, the room enjoys views of the mountains. Affordable materials include wool-blend Berber carpet and painted wood baseboards. The yellow chair is vintage Eames.

are in a certain degree of communication with each other but not lumped together in one huge, open area." To achieve this, he introduced subtle methods of functional separation—for example, a fireplace divides the living and dining rooms, and the kitchen and dining room are delineated with a staircase. "We worked hard to modulate the spaces but not cut them off from each other," he observes.

The home's affordability began in earnest with its floor plan, which was laid out on a two-foot module to accommodate standard size 4 x 8 building materials. This technique kept labor costs as low as possible because there was less trimming and fitting involved, and it reduced waste. Sofield left the floor framing and the underside of the stairway exposed, both as a decorative theme and to save on finishes and trim. In addition, all the floor joists in the house fall on a two-foot module, which facilitated an easy-to-follow floor plan grid that, once again, minimized material quantities and lowered labor expenses.

Affordable exterior features include tempered hardboard siding, one of the least expensive—and most durable—products on the market. Sofield was also attracted to the siding's generous lap width, which balances the verticality of the house and helps preserve its proportions. Inexpensive poured-concrete columns support the porches, whose floors are also poured concrete (as are those of the patios), and exposed rafter tails added depth to the facade and slashed finishing costs. Metal barn roofing was a bargain and, because it reflects solar gain, was an intelligent choice for this high-altitude locale.

Sofield kept the interior materials as inexpensive as possible without sacrificing the aesthetic qualities of the home. He specified Baltic birch plywood flooring and baseboard trim, with wood windows and

The kitchen's dominant feature is its poured-concrete island, stained a copper color to match the concrete floors. The island, which cost just $500, was poured directly onto its own footings, and the house was built around it. Quilted ash veneer plywood cabinets are a minimalist complement to the ceramic tile backsplash. The designer's pet dog, Ray, finds it all to her liking.

baseboards in some rooms, and saved additional money by turning the pieces trimmed from the flooring squares into shelving and a powder room vanity. The kitchen's poured-concrete island, which cost just $500, serves as a spacious work surface and matches the sturdy, low-maintenance concrete slab-on-grade kitchen floors, stained a warm copper color.

In general, Sofield focused on the simplest of finishes and fixtures, steering clear of superfluous ornamentation to create a house that, while unassuming in its demeanor, showcases the successful marriage of architectural exploration and frugality.

The master bedroom, placed at the back of the house for privacy, was given additional square footage with a cantilevered bay pop-out, a technique that didn't break the bank and made the room more spacious. The exposed framing complements the Sheetrock walls, and a walk-in closet sits behind the dresser wall.

The dining area occupies a street-side corner of the house. The corner windows are positioned to allow oblique views of the park across the street while preventing direct views of the table—which is centered in the room—from the sidewalk. The exposed framing continues here, bringing rustic elegance to the room.

Blueprint #7

Striking proof that modernism can find a place in a traditional neighborhood—and that a unique, architect-designed home can be affordable.

Midwest
Ultramodern

St. Paul, Minnesota

Cost per square foot: $115

Architect: Gar Hargens, Close Associates Architects

Photographs: Don F. Wong

WHEN PETER AND JULIE EIGENFELD of St. Paul, Minnesota, asked Gar Hargens to design an ultramodern house in a traditional local neighborhood, the architect was thrilled at the opportunity. "I was excited—they wanted to push the envelope of design, and they had a clear idea of what they wanted and were willing to use any and all materials," he says. "That is an architect's dream. Then, they mentioned their budget."

Hargens, owner of the Minneapolis firm Close Associates Architects, one of the pioneers of modern residential

Budget-Friendly Factors:

—compact floor plan revolves around cube-like forms to reduce corners and overall surface area, making the house more economical to build and cheaper to heat and cool

—prefabricated components: precast ribbed concrete foundation panels used above-grade, stock commercial aluminum window louvers

—Baltic birch plywood, industrial-grade carpet, plastic laminate, Hardiplank siding, Sheetrock, stainless steel nautical cable, vinyl windows, Kalwall translucent fiberglass panel

Cost-conscious materials on the north-facing facade include cedar battens and Hardiplank cement board siding, the longer-lasting and lower-cost alternative to regular plywood, which tends to deteriorate over time. The boards were primed only; not painting them saved money and brought the industrial look the owners wanted. Stainless steel nautical cable adds a contemporary touch to the wood deck.

architecture, had worked with tight budgets before, but the Eigenfelds offered him a tantalizing but intimidating task: hip, modern design combined with good, old-fashioned frugality. The couple had a construction budget of $180,000, and Hargens, accustomed to challenges, went to work.

The architect soon discovered another hurdle: the Eigenfelds had purchased a small 40 x 120-foot lot perched on a bluff with spectacular north-facing views of the Mississippi River Valley and the St. Paul skyline. Notwithstanding its beautiful setting, the lot had a drawback: a 130-foot setback requirement that resulted in an "impacted" and irregularly shaped footprint. Given those parameters, Hargens had to position the house precisely to take full advantage of the allowable building envelope.

Purposefully avoiding complex shapes and angles in order to follow one of the golden rules of architecture—that the precursor to affordability is simplicity—Hargens envisioned two basic box-like

Simple forms, bright colors, and industrial materials combine in a bold display of ultramodern architecture. Silver galvanized corrugated-metal vertical siding catches and reflects light, adding texture to the exterior and visual contrast to the prominent blue corrugated-metal siding. Precast ribbed-concrete foundation panels used above the ground frame the yellow garage door and form the first-level walls.

St. Paul Modern

Lower Level

Bedroom

Bedroom

Stairs to Main Level

Stairs to Main Level

Mechanical

Bathroom

Laundry

Stairs to Entry

Garage Foundation

Main Level

Dining Room

Balcony

Living Room

Stairs to Garden Level

Stairs to Garden Level

Stairs to Living/Dining

Stairs to Upper Level

Stairs to Lower Level

Kitchen

Eating Area

Kitchen Counter Over Half-Bath

Entry

Garage

Tools

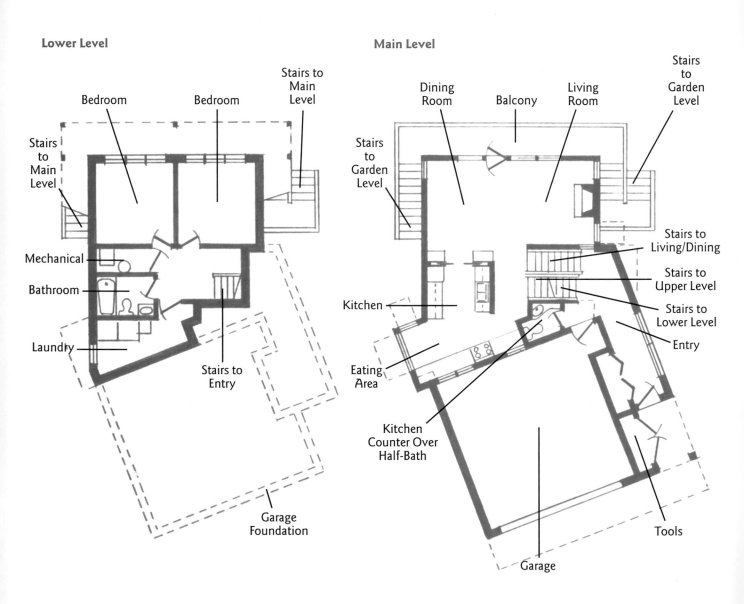

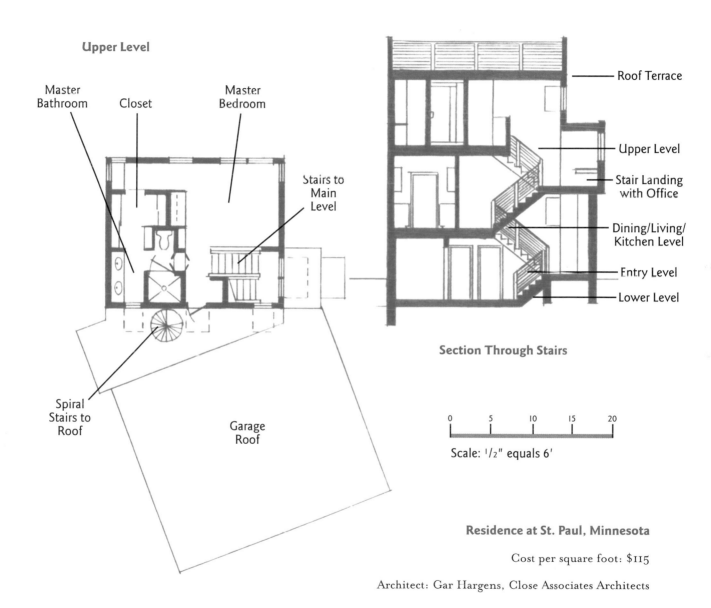

Upper Level

Master
Bathroom

Closet

Master
Bedroom

Stairs to
Main
Level

Spiral
Stairs to
Roof

Garage
Roof

Roof Terrace

Upper Level

Stair Landing
with Office

Dining/Living/
Kitchen Level

Entry Level

Lower Level

Section Through Stairs

0   5   10   15   20

Scale: ¹/₂" equals 6'

Residence at St. Paul, Minnesota

Cost per square foot: $115

Architect: Gar Hargens, Close Associates Architects

Commercial aluminum louvers, factory-painted a classic white and purchased in low-cost off-the-shelf sizes, protect the windows from sunlight and add inexpensive modern detailing to the facade. Standard chassis-style vinyl windows will hold up against the elements and are smart choices for limited budgets. A steel spiral staircase painted a cheerful yellow leads to the roof deck.

The spacious top-level deck offers far-reaching views of the St. Paul skyline and the valley below. The treated wood decking sits over a rubber membrane roof and was applied in sections for easy removal if necessary. The two planters disguise the home's plumbing stack, and the blue metal siding is continued on the inside deck railing.

forms attached at a slight angle to capture the views and adhere to the spatial restrictions of the site. "Keeping the shape of this house as close to a cube as possible reduced the surface area and corners, which made it less expensive to build and easier to heat and cool," he explains.

Located in an older neighborhood of primarily traditional Victorian-style homes, the Eigenfeld house seems to have taken a wrong turn on its way to the California coast. "It is a very interesting addition to this neighborhood," Peter Eigenfeld reports. "There is nothing like it for miles. And the reaction to it has been fun: Some people call it the beach house, or the Swedish flag, because of its colors. Many people drive by slowly, so we know it's getting plenty of attention."

The floor plan of the 1,650-square-foot house progresses from a long, low entry hall up through light-filled interior volumes, culminating in a rooftop deck. Full-height windows and doors and a taller ceiling on the main level work together to further facilitate a feeling of spaciousness, and the stair landings were enlarged to create entry and study space. Despite its compact size, the home has three bedrooms, two-and-a-half bathrooms, a two-car garage, and two decks, proof that economy of space does not have to compromise livability.

One of the home's most dramatic features is its section of silver galvanized corrugated-metal vertical siding, which shimmers in the light, bringing a sense of motion to the structure by catching and reflecting

color from the trees and sky. The refined silver siding contrasts against the home's precast ribbed-concrete foundation panels, rougher in appearance and used above grade in an atypical application for "significant savings," Hargens notes. The panels, which are tornado-resistant and can withstand the harsh temperatures of the Minnesota winter, are commonly specified for below-grade use, but the architect brought them into this home's main exterior palette at a nominal cost and with the allure of easy installation and zero maintenance. Hargens was able to shave thousands from the budget—and weeks from the construction schedule—with this innovative system, which is shipped in pieces and then assembled on-site in a matter of hours. "This modernist technique of finding new applications for materials lowered the overall cost of this house," he says. "The great thing about these materials is that they are as durable as more expensive ones."

A Kalwall translucent fiberglass panel, composed of two sheets of polycarbonate inset with insulation and a painted grid, brings diffused light into the corridor. It was significantly less expensive than a glass window and, as a bonus, provides excellent insulation. The panel was purchased at a substantial discount because it had been sized incorrectly for another building and the company was happy to have it taken off their hands. Other materials in the entry include concrete flooring, rubber matting, Baltic birch plywood cabinetry and trim, and cultured marble—a man-made stone—for the sill.

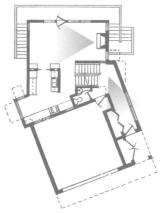

Built-in Baltic birch plywood cabinets, tucked neatly into the living/dining area, don't encroach on the available space, allowing the floor plan to remain small and economical.

A generously sized Baltic birch plywood counter placed over the entry-level powder room serves as a catch-all area and plant bay. The stairway landing is roomy enough for a desk, giving what is often ignored space a useful function without the necessity of additional square footage.

Because the kitchen's burgundy plastic-laminate counters, Baltic birch plywood cabinets and trim, and hanging light fixtures were so inexpensive, more costly target-tread rubber-tile flooring could be worked into the budget for a special design touch.

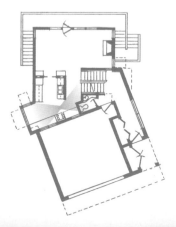

For the interior cabinetry and stair posts, Hargens chose Baltic birch plywood. Although inexpensive, the plywood is so well crafted that its exposed edges can be left unfinished, a technique not recommended for regular plywood. Additional budget-friendly materials include a Kalwall translucent fiberglass panel in the entry hall (the panel was sold as overstock at a greatly reduced price), stock commercial aluminum window louvers (all ten cost just $1,000), Hardiplank cement board siding, vinyl windows, and stainless steel nautical cable for the stairs and deck that the client installed himself. Although the blue metal siding was a splurge, it will prove its economy in the long run because it will last for many years and require only occasional painting.

The house, which took only four months to build, is an outstanding example of affordability and efficiency. "A number of architects I know said we couldn't build this house on this budget," Hargens says. "It helped immensely to have such wonderful clients. I can't say enough about their commitment to helping solve problems, finding and evaluating materials, and keeping their architect on course."

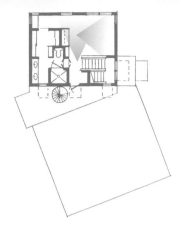

Item of Interest:

The multicolored cabinet unit in the bedroom is from:

Blu Dot Design & Manufacturing, Inc.
3306 Fifth Street NE. Minneapolis, MN 55418
(612) 782-1844
www.bludot.com

A wall cutout above the headboard opens the room to the stair landing, enhancing air circulation and drawing additional ambient light into the space. Although its cost was negligible, the cutout is a functional and aesthetic feature of the room.

The master bedroom's colorful cabinets complement the vinyl windows, kept free of coverings and trimmed only with cultured marble sills. Industrial-grade carpet, used here and throughout the rest of the house, is inexpensive and durable. Cost-conscious Sheetrock was used for all interior walls.

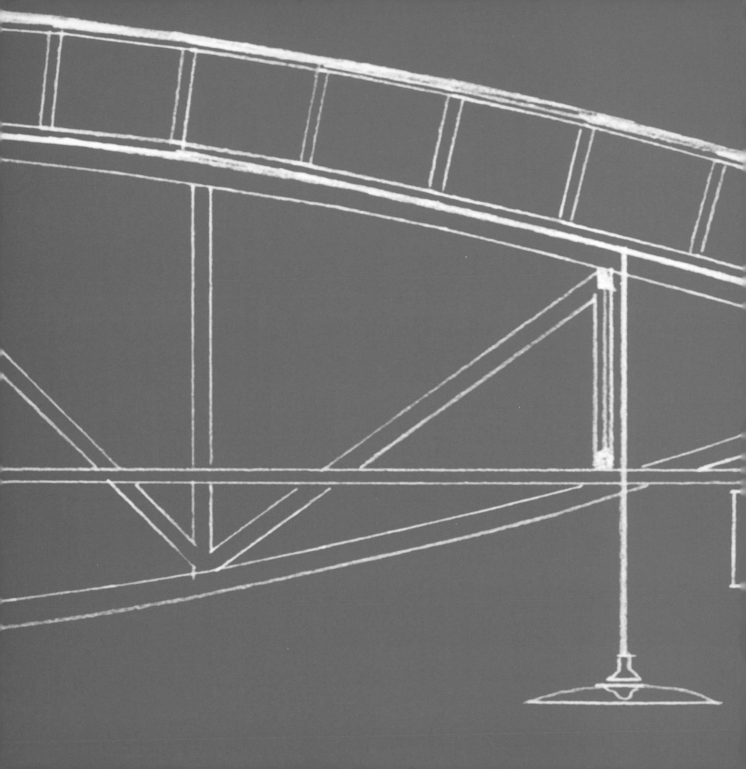

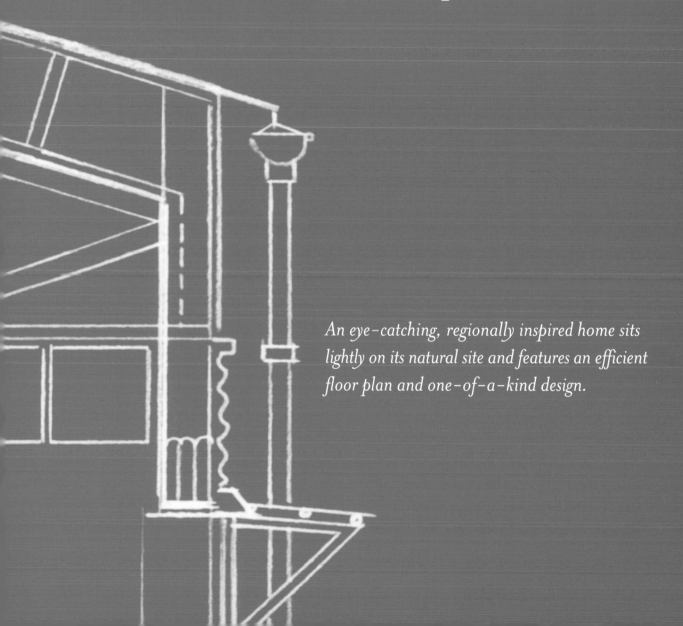

Blueprint #8

An eye-catching, regionally inspired home sits lightly on its natural site and features an efficient floor plan and one-of-a-kind design.

High Design on the Kansas Prairie

Cost per square foot: $125

Architects: Dan Rockhill and David Sain
Rockhill & Associates

Photographs: Dan Rockhill

THE KANSAS LANDSCAPE is imposing, with its vast skies, meaty thunderheads, and persistent expanses of prairie. Architect and University of Kansas professor Dan Rockhill loves the state, and his trained eye can see the beauty that emerges from the plains, sometimes subtly, sometimes with great force. The homes he designs and builds along with his longtime associate, David Sain, are testaments to what can be achieved when there is an alliance between form and place—a sense of effortless belonging and connection.

Budget-Friendly Factors:
—simple rectangular shape based on a pattern of 10-foot bays for consistency and ease of construction

—architects provided a "one-stop" service from design to construction, which removed costs associated with a separate contractor and subcontractors

—concrete, galvanized steel, Sheetrock, corrugated tin, tempered glass, corrugated cement fiberboard siding, cement fiberboard building panels, off-the-shelf lighting fixtures, sliding track doors

Affordable and durable, corrugated cement fiberboard siding in a classic terra-cotta red is an intelligent response to climate extremes, as are cement fiberboard panels, visible here as the smooth gray material beneath the curved roof. Galvanized steel windows and a steel gutter and downspout complement the three-tiered steel brise-soleil, a louver system that shades the house, filters sunlight, and scales down the building.

Rockhill's creation for Barry and Sue Newton reveals this intimacy with the land. "The elementary relationship between the ground and the sky is a continual source of inspiration for our work," he says. "With this house, which sits nestled in the prairie grass, we wanted to give the appearance of an uninterrupted setting, so that the field 'rolls' into the structure. We didn't want it to intrude into the landscape."

Located west of Lawrence, the house conjures up familiar, comfortable images. From some angles, it looks like a little train making its way across the prairie. In other views, its terra-cotta-colored skin echoes the block silos found throughout the region; yet, from other vantage points its shape is reminiscent of the industrial buildings that shelter pumping stations and distribution centers for natural gas and oil. It's all done on purpose, says Rockhill, who begins each project with a meticulous exploration of the site and its history.

Unlike many architectural firms, which put floor plans and details down on paper and then hire builders to convey those ideas, Rockhill's office is a one-stop shop; the only farmed-out work goes to heating and air-conditioning subcontractors. After the drawings and site work are complete, Rockhill and his team roll up their sleeves and get busy—welding trusses; forging windows, doors, and cabinets; pouring concrete; installing siding; and, for this house, sandblasting glass. This hands-on method kept the Newtons' construction costs to $125 per square foot;

The one-story house is structured around a series of 10-foot bays that run the length of the building and suggest a simple, thus cost-effective, floor plan, with rooms positioned along the lines of the bays. The rolled corrugated-steel roof reflects the state's grain bins, which use the same material, and turbine vents on top of the roof spin in the wind and ventilate fresh air through the roof assembly.

Kansas High-Tech

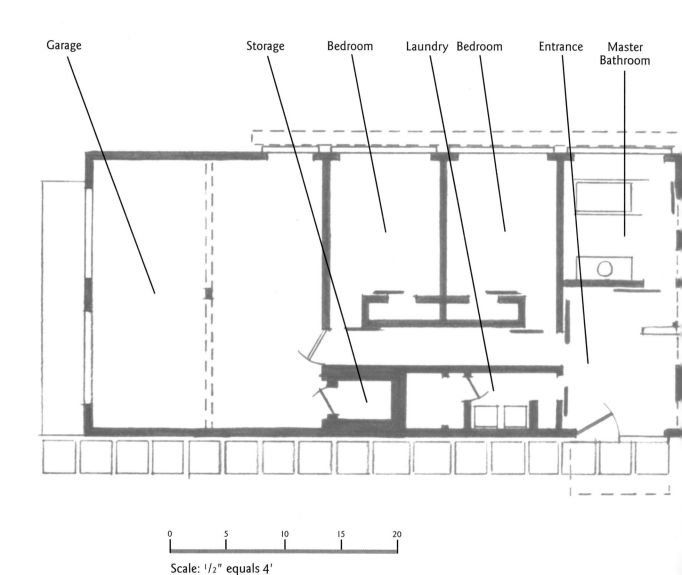

Garage · Storage · Bedroom · Laundry · Bedroom · Entrance · Master Bathroom

Scale: $1/2''$ equals 4'

0   5   10   15   20

Guest
Bathroom   Master
Bedroom   Closets   Kitchen   Living / Dining Area   Screened Porch

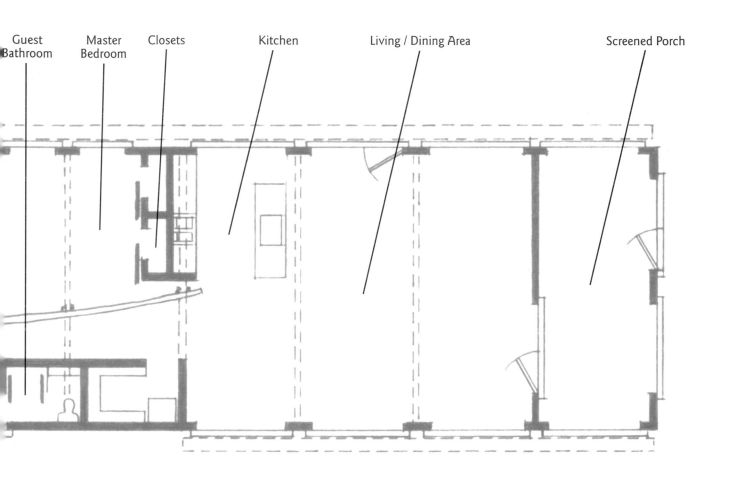

Residence near Lawrence, Kansas

Cost per square foot: $125

Architects: Dan Rockhill and David Sain, Rockhill & Associates

with a traditional approach, they would have paid more.

The simplicity of the Newton residence arises from what Rockhill describes as "a stark agrarian language, which strips the building down to essentials." The long, thin 24 x 110 footprint is divided into 10-foot structural bays that organize the one-story floor plan, which is bracketed by a garage on the south side and a screened porch on the north. The barrel vault roof is made from rolled corrugated steel, a commonly used material that "anchors the house in the region," Rockhill explains. Other budget-friendly and geographically pertinent exterior materials include corrugated cement fiberboard siding, which is extremely durable and easy to maintain; cement fiberboard panels; and a steel brise-soleil—a series of continuous louvers fabricated in Rockhill's shop and placed at evenly spaced intervals along the length of the house to shade it during the summer.

The navigation from the main entry on the east facade to the screened porch passes through spacious, open rooms whose differing functions are delineated by one of the home's most prominent features: an artful curved wall of steel and frosted glass. Overhead, an exposed steel "football" truss supports the roof and imparts an industrial tone to the palette, as does the corrugated tin used for the ceiling. The master bedroom, disguised behind the glass wall, occupies a center bay, and two guest bedrooms are situated closer to the garage end of the home to allow for privacy between the owners and visitors. Floor-to-ceiling windows flood the space with ambient light, and

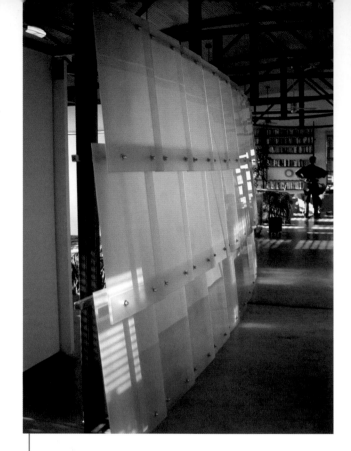

A wall of tempered glass panels, sandblasted for a frosted effect, attached in overlapping layers to a steel frame and fastened together with bolts, brings a feeling of transparency to the interior and captures the light that comes in through the windows. The master bedroom sits behind the glass; a sliding door can close off the room if additional privacy is desired. Located near the center of the floor plan, the wall acts as a transition between the two distinct sections of the house.

The entry wall separates the home's public and private zones, and painted solid-core doors hung on barn-door tracks can be used to open up or close off areas. Standard, low-cost Sheetrock walls provide an unadorned backdrop for artwork; this painting is by the owners' son, Oliver.

inexpensive blinds make it possible to modulate that light as desired.

Because summer temperatures in Kansas can be blistering (Rockhill points out that over 100-degree weather in August is nothing unusual), air circulation was a key concern. If that weren't enough, the winters can bring frigid weather punctuated by formidable winds, so the house had to respond to the extremes of both seasons. Windows positioned high and low on each side of the house take air in and vent it on the opposite side, Rockhill says, amplifying the breezes and creating natural cross-ventilation that helps to cool the interiors, reducing air-conditioning costs. In the winter, the concrete floor absorbs heat from the sun and, because it is supplemented with a cost-effective hot-water heating system embedded in its core, it provides consistent warmth even during the coldest months of the year. Sliding doors can close off sections of the house that aren't being used, making it easier to heat the areas in use. In addition, the home's low profile protects it from the wind; nonetheless, it is equipped with a tornado shelter.

"I give a lot of credit to the Newtons for the way this all came together," Rockhill concludes. "They were open to all possibilities here, and to having a fully custom home they could afford."

Overleaf:

The home's exposed structural steel "football" truss follows the spacing of the 10-foot bay sections. Although more expensive than wood, the truss matches the industrial themes of the design, and its cost was offset by the incorporation of less costly materials, including a corrugated-tin ceiling and concrete floors. The hanging lights were purchased online for just $129 each.

Ample floor-to-ceiling windows are covered with inexpensive blinds that can be used to modulate patterns and quantities of light in the space. An exposed duct, placed high on the wall above the windows, provides a cost-effective way to handle the home's heating and cooling needs. The steel bookcase is a creation of the architects.

Custom steel kitchen cabinets, also by the architects, are fronted with tempered glass and topped with glass counters, and an elegant glass-and-steel island, complete with a cooktop, rounds out the minimal but functional kitchen. To keep the small area uncluttered, the architects placed an under-counter fridge beneath the island and left the walls free of upper cabinets.

Although it looks expensive, the custom glass bathtub, designed by the architects, employs basic materials: aquarium glass set into a galvanized steel frame. The floors are concrete.

Galvanized steel and glass are featured in the guest bathroom. The architects also used recycled black plastic for the sink cabinet.

The home's primary compositional elements—the steel truss and the glass wall—are visible from the master bedroom. The glass sends diffused light and color into the room, and the truss visually lowers the ceiling, making the room more intimate. His-and-her closets made from Sheetrock are equipped with inexpensive sliding track doors.

155

Blueprint #9

Proof that proximity to one of America's most expensive communities doesn't make an affordable, architecturally outstanding house out of the question.

The Colorado Barn, Reinterpreted

Carbondale, Colorado

Cost per square foot: $200

Architect: Scott Lindenau, Studio B Architects

Photographs· Wayne Thom

ALTHOUGH THE TOWN of Carbondale, Colorado, is forty-five minutes away from its glitzy neighbor, Aspen, it feels the effects of the latter's high construction costs. Nonetheless, Brian and Liliann Bailey paid about half the typical going rate in their area for an architect-designed house filled with modern touches, historical cues, and novel applications of affordable materials. (Remember those black work counters in chemistry class? Read on . . .)

Budget-Friendly Factors:

—contractor was closely involved in design process, helping to determine the most affordable route and cost-effective materials

—architect omitted basement from plan, saving thousands on excavation costs; a flat building site brought additional savings

—rusted corrugated-metal siding and roofing, irrigation-pipe columns, salvaged barn-wood siding, recycled courtyard pavement, corrugated Plexiglas, integral-color concrete floors, Fireslate, maple veneer plywood, bamboo, Durarock, Hardiplank wall boards, Kalwall translucent fiberglass panels, prefabricated scissors-truss roof system, sliding barn doors on tracks

The living room end of the house reveals the asymmetrical lines of the overall composition, particularly in the connected shed and gable forms and the angled stone chimney column, capped with a tilted metal panel. The metal shed roof that shelters the patio is supported by 8 x 8 wood timbers, and the wood trellis is held up by irrigation pipes for a budget-friendly way to add visual variation.

To help them realize their dream of a beautiful, budget-friendly home, the Baileys hired Aspen architect Scott Lindenau, a staunch believer that quality architecture should be available to everyone. However, Lindenau didn't have free rein with this project—strict design guidelines forced him to first consider the aesthetic prerequisites of the neighborhood, and later work in attractive low-cost solutions.

Although the guidelines mandated a traditional style of architecture, Lindenau introduced updated interpretations of the agricultural buildings found throughout the region, following the rules but tweaking them to streamline the construction budget and, in the end, capping it at $200 per square foot. "It was a challenge to design a contemporary house in a conservative community like this, but its forms speak to tradition even as they extend aesthetic boundaries," the architect explains. "Because the home is based on old outbuildings and agricultural structures in the valley, and reflects the subdivision's ranch-like setting, the review board gave its approval."

Located on a half-acre plot in River Valley Ranch, a golf course community situated on a flat meadow framed by mountains, this 3,200-square-foot house is a collection of simple gable and shed forms that embrace a sheltered south-facing courtyard that opens to views of the locally famous Mt. Sopris. The home's materials are a studied combination of reclaimed, traditional, and contemporary, all chosen for their affordability, durability, and visual appeal. The house gets its rustic look primarily from 106-year-old barn-wood siding salvaged in Pennsylvania. The siding is a cost-effective choice in the long run

(continued on p. 165)

The front entry reveals the imaginative integration of diverse materials. Irrigation-pipe support columns, corrugated Plexiglas roofing over the recessed doorway, salvaged barn-wood siding, vertical and horizontal slatted siding, rusted metal, rough cedar stairs, light-colored stone, and aluminum-clad windows merge to make a bold statement.

Colorado Barn

Main Level

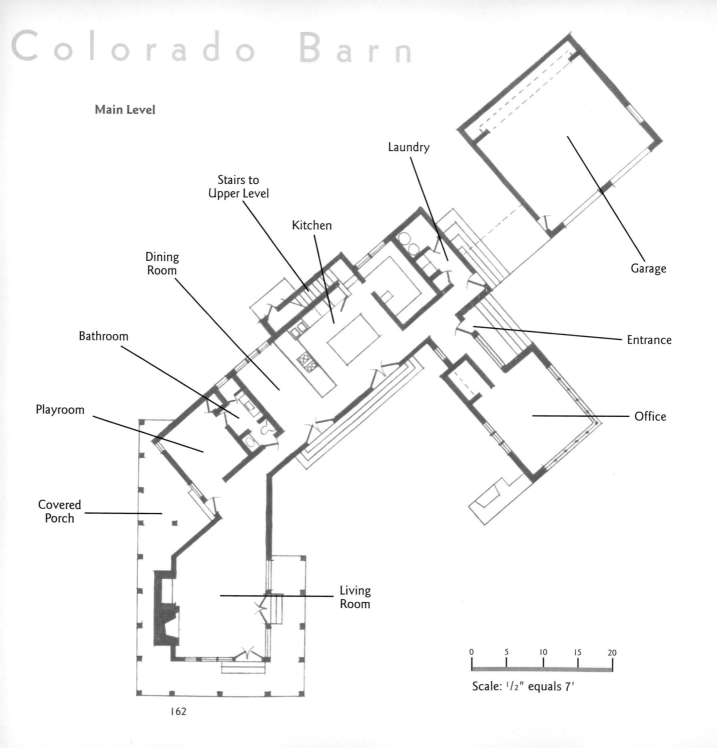

Laundry

Stairs to
Upper Level

Kitchen

Garage

Dining
Room

Bathroom

Entrance

Playroom

Office

Covered
Porch

Living
Room

162

Scale: ¹/₂" equals 7'

0   5   10   15   20

Upper Level

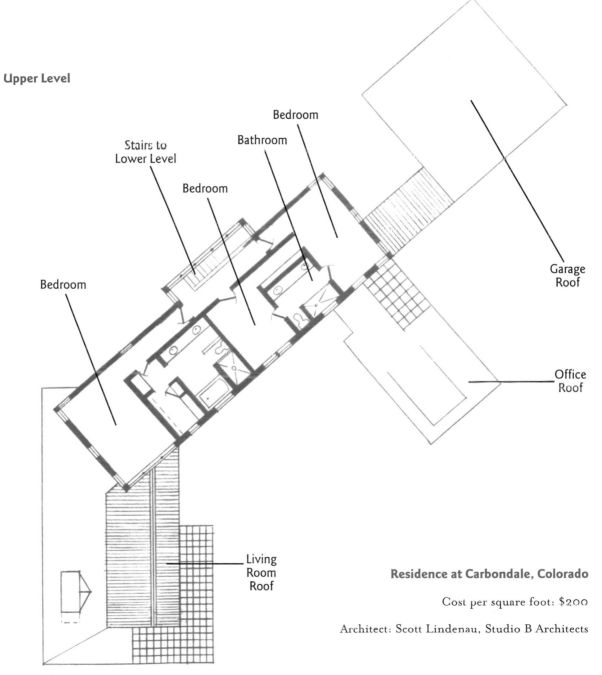

Stairs to Lower Level

Bedroom

Bathroom

Bedroom

Bedroom

Bedroom

Garage Roof

Office Roof

Living Room Roof

Residence at Carbondale, Colorado

Cost per square foot: $200

Architect: Scott Lindenau, Studio B Architects

because it requires less ongoing maintenance than new wood. Other exterior materials include irrigation pipes used as column supports; rusted corrugated metal siding and roofing, which has the added benefit of being able to fend off potential damage from wayward golf balls; rusted metal doors; courtyard pavement formed with chunks of concrete salvaged from a street being torn up in Aspen (the owner found the pieces and laid them himself); corrugated Plexiglas; and stone.

Lindenau gave the house an open floor plan, a technique that minimizes construction costs across the board. Beyond that, the flat building site helped keep the budget on track, and omitting a basement saved thousands on excavation costs. The home's prefabricated scissors-truss roof system proved to be yet another financially savvy measure: assembled on-site, it was much less expensive than a more complex and labor-intensive vaulted ceiling with steel ceiling or ridge beams.

Recessing the front entry created a distinct transition into the home. A custom-designed zinc front door, although relatively more expensive than wood, balances the rustic materials that surround it.

A small window cut into the zinc front door brings daylight into the foyer. Smooth-finish plaster walls supply a clean background for the owners' art collection, and an entry closet made of maple veneer plywood provides unobtrusive storage.

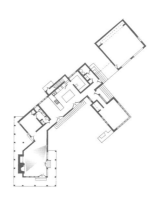

Ecologically sustainable bamboo flooring is less expensive than wood but equally durable. Here, it acts as a natural complement to the integral-color concrete floors in the hallway, as does the affordably priced maple veneer plywood wall. Inexpensive ceiling lights swivel to illuminate artwork.

Featured Artists:

Mark Cesark
(wall hanging on the left)
2130 County Road 102
Carbondale, CO 81623
(970) 704-1830
kmstudio@sopris.net

Gino Hollander
(painting on the right)
979 Queen Street
Aspen, CO 81611
(970) 925-7855
hollander@hollanderart.com

The home's interiors underscore the fact that beauty on a budget is indeed possible. Integral-color concrete floors are less expensive than wood and are easily cleaned (a necessity for mountain living), and durable, ecologically sustainable bamboo flooring installed in the upper-level rooms and living room is about half the price of wood. For the dining room, Lindenau specified Durarock walls—a truly unconventional application. Durarock is typically used as tile underlay in showers, but, as Lindenau points out, "We liked the texture and simplicity of it—and it's inexpensive." In yet another innovative twist, Lindenau used Fireslate for the kitchen counters. A low-cost and surprisingly elegant man-made material, Fireslate was developed for use in chemistry labs but happens to be a smart choice for kitchens because it doesn't

A brushed galvanized-tin fireplace brought casual elegance to the living room without inflating the budget, and a built-in maple veneer plywood entertainment center houses a television and stereo system, blending nicely with the bamboo floors and contemporary furnishings.

Item of Interest:

The leather chairs in the living room are by Montis.

Overleaf:

Douglas fir collar ties support the asymmetrical roof and add a textural element to the modern lines of the living room. Five sets of French doors open to the patio.

scratch and can stand up to the general wear and tear of active family life.

To balance the Durarock and concrete, Lindenau introduced maple veneer plywood to warm the palette and Kalwall translucent panels to filter natural light, then linked the elements with plaster walls, finished entirely flat for a clean, sophisticated appearance.

Brian Bailey acknowledges he wanted to stir up the neighborhood; certainly, he did not want an average solution. "We get a lot of drive-bys," he says. "The house attracts a lot of attention." Adds Lindenau, "The Bailey house proves you can have an architectural home and not spend a fortune."

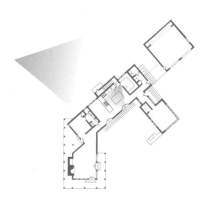

Scratch-resistant and affordable Fireslate counters, originally designed for chemistry labs, work beautifully in a residential setting, and generously sized maple-veneer plywood cabinets and shelves add to the ease and workability of the kitchen. The wall beyond the counter is low-cost Durarock, more typically used as the underlay in showers.

Rusted corrugated metal and barn-wood siding complement each other and impart dramatic contrast to the back of the home. Affordable translucent Kalwall panels bring natural light into the stairway (located in the upper portion of the rusted metal section) and provide privacy.

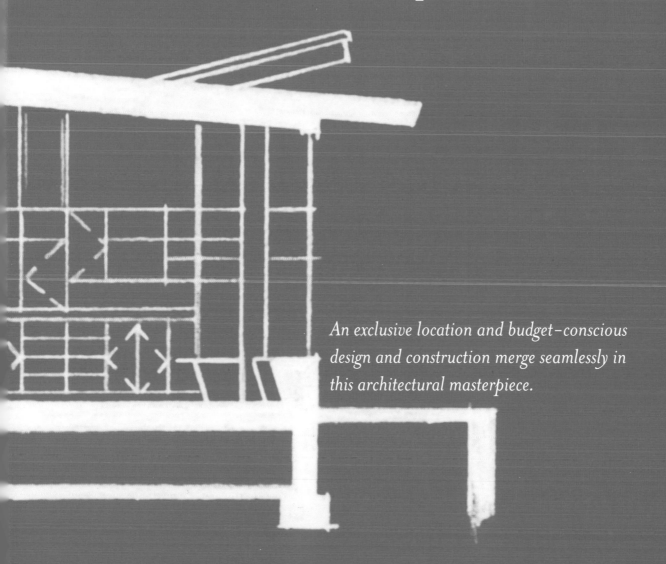

Blueprint #10

An exclusive location and budget-conscious design and construction merge seamlessly in this architectural masterpiece.

Streamlined Sophistication on Martha's Vineyard

Chilmark, Massachusetts

Cost per square foot: $228

Architect: Charles Rose, Charles Rose Architects

Photographs: Chuck Choi

GIVEN THE FOLLOWING circumstances, would a budget-friendly house seem a realistic hope or an impossible dream? Location: one of the most expensive communities in the United States; geography: an island in the Atlantic Ocean; architect: award-winning and increasingly sought after for his site-sensitive, artistic designs.

If your conclusion is that such factors could never add up to a realistic construction budget, you will be pleasantly surprised: This extraordinary home in the town of Chilmark on Martha's Vineyard was built for a comparatively low-cost $228 per square

Budget-Friendly Factors:

—spare building technology and an open, single-level floor plan characterized by modest detailing throughout

—owner stayed closely involved during design and construction process, so was able to track expenses as they surfaced

—exposed concrete foundation, wood windows in stock sizes, western red cedar, yellow cedar, mahogany, powder-coated steel, aluminum, poured-in-place concrete, nautical cable, beech veneer, maple casework

The home's plentiful glass acts like a "wrapper" that visually connects the indoor and outdoor spaces, creating a sense of transparency throughout the home, as illustrated in this view to the courtyard. Maple casework and beech flooring are affordable and beautiful materials.

foot. "This was a client with a deliberately modest budget who wanted custom architecture and was very serious about how money would be spent," says architect Charles Rose of Charles Rose Architects.

Part of why the client, who had worked in the construction profession, was able to keep the budget in check had to do with his own building experience, as well as his hands-on involvement in the project from the initial design planning through construction and the final finishing stages. Flexibility was imperative in this situation, Rose explains, pointing out that owner, architect, and contractor worked as a unit to alter or rethink the home's specifications as the work progressed— and, most importantly, as the budget dictated. "The contractor had to justify every expense," says Rose.

Knowing that architectural complexity will inflate a construction budget, Rose's first step was to give the house a one-level floor plan that allows it to embrace its lush setting and offer comfortable living spaces that resonate with a decidedly down-to-earth feel. This approach, the alternative to stacking floors on multiple levels, was a smart money-saving technique. The result is a dwelling—organic in texture and tone, low-slung and understated—that sweeps gracefully across its treed site.

At approximately 2,800 square feet, the home is relatively small compared to many others on the island, although its unfettered layout gives it a larger appearance. "Limiting the
(continued on p. 184)

The low-slung house nestles into its wooded setting, and separate wings for guests (left) and a master bedroom (right) offer privacy within the one-story floor plan, which places the main living areas between the two wings. An L-shaped deck follows the form of the house, and an indoor/outdoor fireplace lends a strong verticality to the facade.

Deck

Stairs to Garden

Bedroom

Bathroom

Bedroom

Bedroom

Outdoor Shower

Laundry

Bathroom

Bedroom

Kitchen

Sunroom

Deck

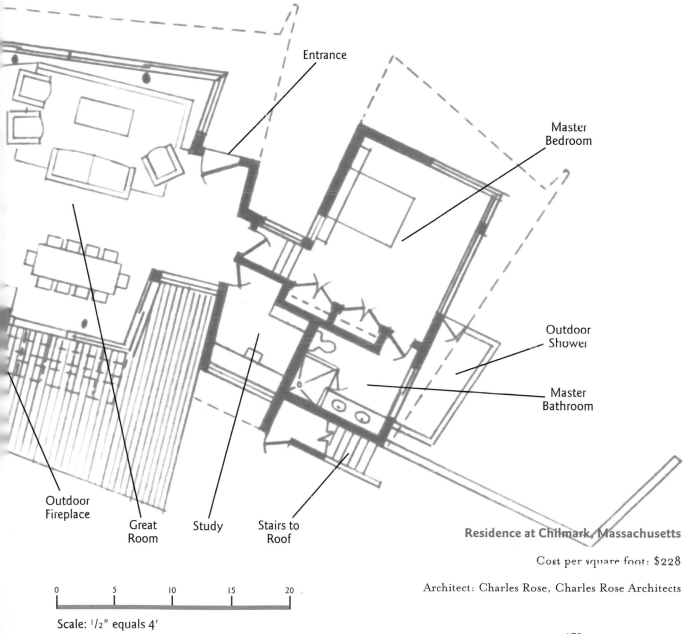

Entrance

Master
Bedroom

Outdoor
Shower

Master
Bathroom

Outdoor
Fireplace

Great
Room

Study

Stairs to
Roof

Residence at Chilmark, Massachusetts

Cost per square foot: $228

Architect: Charles Rose, Charles Rose Architects

0   5   10   15   20

Scale: $^1/_2$" equals 4'

The home's materials blend seamlessly and are an exercise in meticulous detailing, as shown in this view of the front entry. The 4-inch steel support post to the left is clad in fir and has a shape reminiscent of a ship's mast—a nod to local seafaring history. Yellow cedar window trim and cedar for the overhangs are inexpensive, long-lasting choices. Leaving the concrete foundation exposed rather than cladding it was a clever money-saving technique that also brought variation to the exterior.

An economical poured-in-place concrete chimney and fireplace surround anchor the spacious deck and connect the exterior and interior spaces. The south-facing cedar trellis, supported by a galvanized steel structure, shades the house from high-angle sun during the summer and allows sunlight to warm the interior spaces during the winter. This corner of the house opens fully to the deck, as do the doors to a small sitting room (left). Western red cedar for exterior walls and mahogany for the deck provide durability and beauty.

Overleaf:

Slim rectangular clerestory windows allow additional light into the sitting room, which opens completely to the deck thanks to generous fixed-glass sliding doors. Although the doors were relatively more expensive than other features in the home, keeping their glass fixed rather than operable reduced their cost.

Budget-friendly aluminum and inexpensive nautical cable form the deck railing, contributing a delicate and airy balance to the predominantly wood exterior. The roof system was designed to collect rainwater and discharge it from scuppers. The roof's cantilevered overhangs also form the porch, a cost-conscious technique that eliminates the need for additional porch support elements.

square footage kept the budget within reach," Rose says. "The first thing to do when cost is a consideration is control the size of the house. Ask yourself how you can minimize the area of the structure, and consider multi-use spaces." In another cost-conscious move, Rose placed most of the house on a crawl space instead of a full basement—a very inexpensive way to build.

The home is characterized by what Rose describes as "a sense of transparency," an effect achieved through the generous placement of large wood windows and doors, some of which open fully to the outdoors, linking the interiors visually and physically to the exterior elements. "The windows are beautiful but modest—they only look expensive," the architect points out. "Although they're perhaps not as large as what you could get with higher-cost, custom-sized systems, they work well in this house, were easy on the budget, and create a strong connection to the landscape."

When it came to pinching pennies, the Chilmark house was also an exercise in what not to include. For example, the owner wasn't compelled to spend money on a high-tech media system or fancy appliances and light fixtures, but the result proves it is possible to build a

A multifunctional great room such as this one, which combines the kitchen, dining, and living room areas, eliminates the need for dividing walls, thus lowering building costs. Additional money-saving techniques in the kitchen included keeping the space small and combining less-expensive open shelving with closed cabinets. The concrete fireplace adds textural contrast to the room, and plaster walls create a clean backdrop for the home's materials. Because of the abundance of natural light, light fixtures were installed sparingly—and money was saved.

quality home and finish it with standard, off-the-shelf items. In the same vein, keeping the building technology of the house simple (for example, using a minimal amount of steel and only where needed, such as for structural cantilevers and flying roofs) further trimmed the budget.

When it came time to decide what to include, the goal was clearly stated: find materials that are affordable, aesthetic, and, whenever possible, native to the island to save money on transportation. In this house, solid beech and beech veneer, cedar, mahogany, poured-in-place concrete, granite, aluminum, and

powder-coated steel (in lieu of more expensive stainless steel) combine inside and out to compose a home that, while modestly detailed, exudes a high level of craftsmanship. The home's copper roof was "marginally more expensive than other roofing materials," Rose says, "but it adds a lot to the house aesthetically and in terms of life cycle."

For Rose, the challenge of building a beautiful home on a budget is one he embraces—and enjoys. "A lavish budget is not a requirement," he says, pointing out that resourcefulness, creativity, and a keen appreciation for value will take you far. Judging by the Chilmark house, he is absolutely correct.

Here, various pieces of the interior palette converge to foster an effect of visual richness and to highlight the level of craftsmanship found throughout the home. Even structural elements, such as the fir-clad steel support column, become aesthetic features thanks to the careful selection and application of materials.

The clean lines of the beech veneer cabinetry and no-frills granite counters impart an affordable elegance to the room, which is characterized by a juxtaposition of materials and elements: generously sized windows; a fir-clad structural column; a granite-topped windowsill that doubles as a seat; an exterior overhang clad in cedar, a material that continues on the interior ceiling; and an open kitchen shelf, supported by a thin cable, that emphasizes the home's transparency by extending across the corner window.